THE ART OF

Caring
Leadership

• • •

THE ART OF

Caring

Leadership

• • •

How Leading with Heart
Uplifts Teams and
Organizations

Heather R. Younger

Berrett–Koehler Publishers, Inc.

Berrett-Koehler Publishers, Inc.
1333 Broadway, Suite 1000
Oakland, CA 94612-1921
Tel: (510) 817-2277
Fax: (510) 817-2278
www.bkconnection.com

ORDERING INFORMATION
Quantity sales. Special discounts are available on quantity purchases by corporations, associations, and others. For details, contact the "Special Sales Department" at the Berrett-Koehler address above.
Individual sales. Berrett-Koehler publications are available through most bookstores. They can also be ordered directly from Berrett-Koehler: Tel: (800) 929-2929; Fax: (802) 864-7626; www.bkconnection.com.
Orders for college textbook / course adoption use. Please contact Berrett-Koehler: Tel: (800) 929-2929; Fax: (802) 864-7626.

Distributed to the U.S. trade and internationally by Penguin Random House Publisher Services.

Berrett-Koehler and the BK logo are registered trademarks of Berrett-Koehler Publishers, Inc.

Printed in the United States of America

Berrett-Koehler books are printed on long-lasting acid-free paper. When it is available, we choose paper that has been manufactured by environmentally responsible processes. These may include using trees grown in sustainable forests, incorporating recycled paper, minimizing chlorine in bleaching, or recycling the energy produced at the paper mill.

Library of Congress Cataloging-in-Publication Data

Names: Younger, Heather R., author.
Title: The art of caring leadership : how leading with heart uplifts teams
    and organizations / Heather R. Younger.
Description: First edition. | Oakland, CA : Berrett-Koehler Publishers, Inc.,
    [2021] | Includes index.
Identifiers: LCCN 2020051895 | ISBN 9781523092147 (paperback) |
    ISBN 9781523092154 (adobe pdf) | ISBN 9781523092215 (epub)
Subjects: LCSH: Leadership. | Caring. | Teams in the workplace.
Classification: LCC HD57.7.Y72 2021 | DDC 658.4/092—dc23
LC record available at https://lccn.loc.gov/2020051895

First Edition

27 26 25 24 23 22 21   10 9 8 7 6 5 4 3 2

Cover design: Adam Johnson. *Interior design and composition:* Leigh McLellan Design. *Copyeditor:* Elissa Rabellino. *Proofreader:* Mary Hazlewood. *Indexer:* Ken Dellapenta. *Chapter opening illustration:* Michael Starkman.

• • •

For my sweet children—
Gabriela, Sebastian, Dominic, and Matteo
—who help me show care

Contents

• • •

● ● ●

There are many employees in the world who are in pain.
They are in pain because they are seeking leaders
who care about them, not for what they can do
but for who they are and can become.

For the leaders who want to commit to
growing in compassion and showing more care
for those they lead, your journey starts here.

Foreword

• • •

I met Heather in a very digital way. In fact, we have never met in person! You see, we have a mutual friend, Garry Ridge, chairman and CEO of the amazing WD-40 Company, and I post simple gratitude photos every day on LinkedIn. I saw Heather's work and was impressed with her passion and dedication. She invited me to be a guest on her podcast, and we are now connected in a very meaningful way. Her whole mission is to guide leaders to a way of leading where caring is at the center of all they do. It's not just what she does, it is who she is at her very core.

I could relate because I had a caring leader early in my career who changed my life, simply because he understood what Heather teaches so well: that by caring, we can do remarkable things together.

Here is my story.

I remember the call like it was yesterday.

My CEO at the time, Kent Murdock, called me about writing a book on employee recognition. I was a regional salesperson at the time, and about a year before, we had had a conversation about how we as a recognition company should become the thought leaders in our industry, and that the way to do that was to publish the definitive book on employee recognition.

You see, I thought that it would make my life easier if people called me instead of my having to cold-call them. Kent thought it was a great idea and challenged me to write the book. "Whoa! I didn't mean I should write the book! My idea was that the company should write the book and I should benefit from said book." That was when Kent said a few words that would change my life. He said, "Chester, you are a smart guy. Figure it out."

Well, for about the next year I played with titles and ideas and what the book should look like. I wasn't making much progress. (I was a busy sales guy with a crushing quota.) So, when Kent called again, I was surprised that he had even remembered the idea. He said, "We just hired a new head of Communications. His name is Adrian Gostick. He is a writer. Introduce yourself to him at the next sales meeting and write the book!"

Twenty-plus years later, together we have written twelve books on recognition and employee engagement and culture together. Many have been *New York Times* and *Wall Street Journal* best sellers. We have sold more than 1.5 million copies and have traveled to more than fifty countries helping leaders and organizations create teams and cultures where people believe that what they do matters, that they make a difference, and when they do, someone celebrates their contributions. It has been a wonderful mission, and I hope it has changed the lives of leaders and organizations all over the world for the better. It all happened because at a critical point in time, I had a caring leader.

Kent could have easily forgotten about the idea or even had someone else write the book. Instead, he created a way for Adrian and me not only to write but to flourish! Because he cared about me and my development, my life changed, and the direction of the company changed in many ways. A lot of things got better for a lot of people, all because Kent Murdock understood the effect that a leader could have on just one person, me. He understood the *art* of being a caring leader, and I am forever grateful.

I tell you this story because the purpose of this amazing book by my good friend Heather Younger is to give *you* the road map to becoming a caring leader—a leader who makes a difference in the lives of the people who follow you and, by extension, the team, their customers, and especially their families. You see, I have never met a caring leader whose impact stopped at work. It always rippled into their families and communities. Isn't that beautiful?

I hope you will take the time to read and study what Heather shares with you in *The Art of Caring Leadership*. It is well researched and carefully written to help you become the leader you need to be for your people and yourself. If there is one thing we all learn in our lives and in our trials, it's that when we care for each other, everything gets better. It is all laid out for you, right here. All you have to do is commit, and start reading!

May your leadership journey be filled with opportunities to put caring at the center of everything you do.

With gratitude,
Chester Elton
Best-selling author of *Leading With Gratitude*, *All In*, and *The Carrot Principle*
The Apostle of Appreciation!

Preface

• • •

Like most of you reading this book, I have had managers who genuinely cared for me and those who did not. Those who did not genuinely care for me left me feeling taken for granted and like I was a number. Those few who made me feel cared for did so by making me feel that I had an important role to play in the success of the team and the organization.

Because I am an empathetic person who deeply values the contributions of others, employees, whether directly or indirectly on my team, would often sit with me and share their concerns about their managers and the culture. Often, I would hear things like, "I don't understand why they do not care about all my efforts" or "They don't care about the hours I work; they just want me to get the work done." Conversely, I remember employees often telling me, "I love being on this team, as I can tell that the leadership team cares about us" or "I really appreciate receiving the recognition of my manager, because it makes me feel cared for and like what I do matters."

Since 2015, my professional focus has been as an employee advocate. More specifically, my consulting practice primarily focuses on what I refer to as "Voice of the Employee" work. What do I mean by this? I help organizational leaders listen more effectively to what their employees want and help them use that truth in productive ways. My firm does this by scouring employee engagement and culture surveys for common themes that leaders can use to drive their culture and engagement forward in a positive direction. We also do this by convening and facilitating culture teams, focus groups, employee resource groups (ERGs), and affinity groups.

After what seemed like a lifetime of hearing and reading about the types of scenarios described above and experiencing them myself, I felt that I needed to clearly define what caring leadership looked like. That background is the inspiration for this book.

Although I am the only credited author of this book, *The Art of Caring Leadership* draws its content from an archive of my personal interviews with leaders of all backgrounds from different parts of the world on my *Leadership With Heart* podcast. It's also inspired by my research and review of direct employee feedback. It highlights the strengths, trials, and practical advice of caring leaders on what they did to become leaders who are more attuned to themselves and how they impact those around them. This book's contents include key points pulled from each interview along with my observations, takeaways, and strategies. You will be able to refer to the Guest Appendix at the end of the book to find out a little more about each person whom I both interviewed on my podcast and included in this book.

I include a section at the end of each chapter titled, "The Art of Caring Leadership in Practice," which highlights the practical learning or takeaways from that chapter.

Then, at the end of the book, I invite you, via an assessment link, to complete a free Caring Leadership self-assessment. The assessment and corresponding report will act as a blueprint for filling any gaps you might have in expressing care more often, much like the popular Strengths-Finder assessment. You might consider working through the results with a coach to help affirm the best route to take for sustained change. To enable greater accountability in working to fill those gaps, I have also created a Caring Leadership online community, facilitated and monitored by me or someone on my team, where "caring leaders in development" can congregate for mutual feedback and support. You will have access to many other resources in that community.

This book is meant for managers, anyone who considers himself or herself a leader, those who coach and consult with managers and/or leaders, anyone who might train managers and/or leaders, and anyone who wants to learn how to express care more often. Those who read this book will get an instant boost to their emotional intelligence, become more aware of themselves and others, and realize the positive power they possess to change the experience of those they lead simply by showing that they care.

The more that leaders express care for those they lead, the more those who follow them will feel that care and go over and above, out of loyalty and deep gratitude, for the benefit of that leader, that team, and the organization. This is as compelling a reason as I can think of to pursue the art of caring leadership. Enjoy!

Care deeply,
Heather R. Younger, JD
Colorado
August 31, 2020

So, You Think You're a Caring Leader?

• • •

No one cares how much you know,
until they know how much you care.
Theodore Roosevelt

"**Caring leadership is** more art than science." I heard this come out of the mouths of those I interviewed for this book many times. Why art? When we think of art, we might think of creativity, fluidity, flexibility, and beauty in between the strokes. When do we know that the artist has completed his or her creation? When we experience it through our senses, and our hearts sing. The same is true for caring leadership.

Just as beauty is in the eye of the beholder, so too is the follower the one who knows and judges whether his or her leaders care. This is not a cookie-cutter approach to becoming a leader who cares. In fact, in my almost one hundred interviews for this book, not everyone exhibited care in the exact same way. Just as we might think of Monet and Picasso as artists with different styles, each leader practices leadership in his or her own unique way.

Merriam-Webster defines *caring* as "feeling or showing concern for or kindness to others."[1] How do I define *leadership*? I often use the words *manager* and *leader* interchangeably in that those who report to us or look to us for guidance think of us as their boss or manager. No matter our title, *leadership* to me is a verb and requires an intention to help someone's life be better and the commitment to act for the benefit of others.

For the purposes of this book, then, *caring leadership* is taking daily actions in ways that show concern and kindness to those we lead.

I discovered what caring leadership looked like when I was a young child. I am the product of an interracial and interfaith marriage. My mom is White and Jewish, and my dad is Black and Christian. I grew up celebrating holidays and traditions from both backgrounds, which contributed to my ability to navigate complex relationships. Explicitly excluded from any public family gatherings by my maternal grandparents, I was literally the black sheep of my family, because of what I looked like. This often left me feeling that I was not worthy, that I was not good enough, that my voice did not matter to the adults in my life (more on this in chapter 9).

When I was nine, my mom and dad decided to move us across the country from Ohio to live in Las Vegas, where my dad would be a stagehand at a large hotel. To keep me connected to the Hanukkah tradition, which was a bright spot in my childhood, my mother's youngest sister, who had remained in Ohio, began sending me a huge box with eight individually wrapped gifts that I was to open every day of the Hanukkah celebration. I remember staring at that large box with anticipation every year I received it. It was a sign of connection to that side of the family and a symbol of my relationship with the other half of myself.

My aunt, whom I looked to as a leader, had a special way of making me feel included, even as an outsider. She was hyper-focused on making me feel that I was worthy of her love and affection, that I was an important member of the family. As a result, she held a special place in my heart. While she probably did not know it at the time, her consistent efforts to show me concern and kindness made her a caring leader. She was a bright light for me in a family that never seemed to truly care about how I felt.

I have had just a few other caring leaders in my life, including my own mother, who chose to stay on a bumpy path by marrying my father and loving me unconditionally despite being ostracized by her family and friends for the union.

Much later in my journey, I encountered three other leaders who, without knowing it, touched my heart and made me feel that I mattered, and that my efforts inside the workplaces where I worked had impact and meaning to them, my team, customers, and the greater community.

It was through the simple daily actions of this handful of leaders, combined with my painful journey of exclusion, that my style of leadership was born. I set out over the years to make sure that those I led felt worthy, that they mattered in a big way, that I was invested in their future, and that they were important, not for what they did for me but in and of themselves.

I experienced deep loyalty from those who were on my teams. They knew I cared for them, and they would go over and above to ensure the success of our team's initiatives and goals. We achieved much together; they delighted customers and met timelines. Even after I was no longer their manager, we held a close bond that was undeniable.

Over the years, I also met leaders whom I chose not to emulate. I saw the negative impacts of their words, their actions, and their inactions. Employees, on and off my team, asked me for advice and wondered what made their leaders act the way they did. I could feel their pain. Their pain and confusion immediately triggered in me those same feelings I had had as a child and young adult of not feeling worthy, not having a voice, not feeling that I mattered. I knew I had to do something about it. I had to use my gifts born out of my journey to benefit those who felt as I did, and I also needed to help change the hearts and minds of leaders everywhere. This background is why I am doing the work that I do now.

Every leader thinks that he or she is a caring leader, and the majority want to be caring leaders, but most fall short of demonstrating that care in consistent ways. This book helps leaders bring to life that desire to care by providing a blueprint they can use to genuinely express that care in very definitive ways. It takes something that is often a nebulous concept or attitude and presents concrete ways to demonstrate care. The precepts in this book go beyond the normal kind words and the niceties that the word *care* often conjures up. Just the opposite, this book is a sort of master plan for any leader who strives to be known as a leader who cares or as a leader with heart.

What Does Becoming a Caring Leader Mean in This Context?

It starts with leaders actually *caring for* those we lead. Caring for people means that we care for them for their own good. We are committed to seeing them succeed for themselves, not just for what they can do for us or our team or organization. We put selfishness aside and look to raise them up to help them grow. In a very real way, we "love" them for just being them.

As Brent Stockwell, assistant city manager of the city of Scottsdale, Arizona, so eloquently professed in our interview, "Just as parents do and families, we need to have love and care for our organizations to help the people we work with be successful."

Which Behaviors Contradict Caring Leadership?

There are leaders who self-proclaim that they are caring leaders, but it is baseless and not genuine. They show very little concern or kindness to those who look to them for leadership and guidance. Often, they use words only and fail to back up those words with the proper expression of care as I define in this book. These leaders leave their people feeling battered and taken for granted, as though what they have to offer means nothing to the organization.

The caring leader is not the manager who never responds to an employee when he makes a request. The caring leader is not the manager who goes out of her way to keep her employee from advancing in his career. The caring leader is not the manager who micromanages every little thing, leaving her employees feeling squeezed away from independent thinking and action. The caring leader is not the manager who shows favoritism and excludes certain members of the team. The caring leader is not someone who is aware that his employees are hurting but responds with "I don't care. The only thing that matters is that you get your job done!"

The phrase *caring leader* can feel vague. To the contrary, every employee intuitively knows whether or not she is cared for by those who she considers her bosses or managers. She knows it, not just because of the leader's words, but more for his actions and how those actions leave her feeling.

Why Would Any Leader Want to Become a Caring Leader?

Every leader thinks about his impact on the bottom line, promotions, and saving face when making decisions. There is great pressure to care about return on investment and focus on projects and tasks, but the leaders I refer to in this book understand that caring for those they lead ensures success in all other areas. They know this because these leaders see how their people respond to them when they behave in line with the principles in this book and when they fail to do so.

Employees are the ones who execute on strategic initiatives and organizational goals. Employees' zest to reduce costs and increase focus or meet customer needs and be a good teammate is exponentially higher if they feel cared for by those who lead them.

How Does One Become a Caring Leader?

The first step to becoming a caring leader is to want to make a change in leadership behavior. Most leaders will not be looking to change unless there is some type of catalyst or driver. Often, this is in the form of performance review results, 360 assessment results, employee engagement survey results for their particular department, a major life change like being fired from a job, high turnover, the need to complete a large project, or the need to increase employee performance.

The leader either is self-aware of some deficiency and wants to improve, is aware of the deficiency and doesn't think he needs to improve, or is oblivious to the deficiency. Once he is self-aware and also wants to change, that is when he is primed to become a caring leader.

No leader fully arrives at a destination labeled "Caring Leader," but those who report to them immediately feel the positive impact of the shifts in behavior. Therefore, caring leadership is an art form where the leader consistently adds different brushstrokes to her behaviors to elicit more positive emotions in those she leads.

In short, the caring leader who excels in the domain of *soft skills*—a term often used to refer to skills, aptitudes, and attitudes such as integrity, communication, empathy, compassion, courtesy, responsibility, social skills, a positive attitude, professionalism, flexibility, teamwork, and strong work ethic—produces hard-core results that drive the business forward. The leaders I highlight in this book either have been handpicked by me for displaying many of these soft skills or were referred to me by listeners of my *Leadership With Heart* podcast who recognized those traits and felt compelled to make introductions.

I specifically excluded individual contributors as guests on my podcast because I wanted to focus on those who lead a team, whether it has one member or two hundred. Accordingly, my conversations were less about where they work than how they show up for those they lead when at work.

Leaders who intentionally exercise their power to be more emotionally intelligent in their communications and interactions show much more heart in the process. This display of heart keeps their team members and coworkers bonded to them and drives increased employee engagement and loyalty. As Karen Johnson, equity and inclusion administrator at the Washington Department of Corrections, said during our interview, "If you take care of your staff, if you take care of the people that are entrusted to your care, they will not only take care of the people that they are supposed to take care of, they will also take care of you."

Is There a Way to Measure Care?

It is often said that "what gets measured, gets managed." I would change this statement to say, "Where change is important, it should get measured." Over the last twelve years, I have measured both customer and employee feedback. While I don't consider myself a data person, when it comes to gauging the sentiment of employees, I am more than happy to dive into both quantitative and qualitative data. I use data to get to the truth. In my business, the truth is what drives increased employee engagement, employee retention, and profitable organizations.

Since 2015, I have personally reviewed over twenty thousand employee survey comments and facilitated almost one hundred focus groups, or culture team meetings. This is not hyperbole. My team and I continue to do this work because getting to the truth by helping organizations listen more effectively to their employees is worth the analysis. For years, I have helped organizations measure employee sentiment on a variety of topics. I have seen the themes. This knowledge serves as a basis for this book. It also allowed me to aggregate the behaviors of the leaders I interviewed.

After you read this book, I invite you to complete the first step of measuring your level of care in the form of a proprietary "Caring Leadership Self-Assessment" (an invitation by this name with a web link is in the back of the book). There will be more tools that I will introduce as we go. If it is important to you that those you lead know that you truly care about them, then it is worthwhile to express that care, increase that care, and measure how they perceive your level of care. You think you are already a caring leader? Let's make sure of that together. You will learn how to measure that more effectively in chapter 10.

How Is This Book Organized?

The Art of Caring Leadership has nine interdependent chapters to guide readers as outlined below. I say "interdependent" because while each caring leader behavior can stand on its own and help any leader improve his relationship with his people, the real art comes when leaders focus their energy on exhibiting their own special combination of them all. Readers will see this synergy in action in this book.

I have included quotes and/or stories from those whom I interviewed on my podcast. For a good reference, I have also included an appendix with a little more about each of the referenced leaders.

After reading through almost one hundred transcripts from my interviews on my podcast over the last two and a half years, I realized that I must start with a chapter on self-leadership. One cannot begin to show caring leadership to others if she does not care for or lead herself first. Therefore, I chose to focus on that topic in chapter 1. If we liken self-leadership to an artist's tool kit, then we realize that the elements of self-leadership are just as a paintbrush, palette, canvas, and clay are to an artist. They are the starting point with which art becomes a reality.

The remaining nine chapters of the book are organized less in order of importance and more in an order consistent with how many of the leaders I interviewed exhibited the specific behaviors. Each chapter begins with a description of the particular aspect of caring leadership and evidence supporting its importance; continues with a firsthand experience, focusing on a caring leader behavior; gives examples for how to practice the aspect of caring leadership; and presents a highlight from someone who embodies this aspect of caring leadership.

Remember, caring leadership means taking daily actions in ways that show concern and kindness to those we lead. The principles in this book that help us get there are timeless. The following describes how the chapters are organized to help us more easily access the daily actions required to become a caring leader:

Chapter 1: Cultivate Self-Leadership Skills. Self-leadership is a critical focus for the caring leader, in that if he is not able to care for himself first, he cannot properly care for those he leads. This involves understanding the purpose and reason for leading; having control over one's mindset; having a coach or mentor; and simply taking time to care for one's mind, body, and spirit.

Chapter 2: Make Them Feel Important. Many employees don't feel seen by those who are supposed to lead them. The caring leader makes sure to set time with her people one-on-one and listens intently to what her employees need from her to do their best work. When this type of leader is around, employees feel as if they are the only one who matters. Employees feel a deep bond with this type of leader, because they feel that they can be their best selves and they are appreciated for the work they put in.

Chapter 3: Look for the Greatness in Those We Lead. Caring leaders get it when it comes to recognizing and then growing the gifts and talents of those they lead. Instead of ignoring the signs of greatness in their people, these leaders search it out. Then they go out of their way to leverage the gifts of those they lead. They meet with their people to ask what they can do for them instead of expecting performance without the proper care.

Chapter 4: Involve Them. Often leaders feel that the problems facing the business are theirs to solve alone. When they tell their employees about the issues they are facing, leaders see that they don't have to conquer the problems alone. In fact, when they involve their employees in overcoming whatever might be facing them, it brings the team closer together. They learn to rely on one another and get more accomplished together. Most important, they endear their employees to them even more, because the leader shows that he or she is human.

Chapter 5: Lead the Whole Person. Many leaders handle employees with the narrow lens of their performance inside the workplace without ever considering them as whole people with lives outside of work. The caring leader understands that to get the most out of his relationships with those he leads, he must consider his employees' lives in aggregate, including what is happening in their lives outside of work. This might mean helping them deal with mental health issues, brainstorming with them on which way to go with a child, or various other personal issues. Caring leaders don't separate the person from what might be happening to her. To the contrary, they meet their employees where they are to help them achieve and be more.

Chapter 6: Create a Listening Culture. The caring leader uses the voices of her people to improve the workplace for all. These leaders know that listening by itself is not enough. Employees feel powerful when they know that their feedback will be acted upon, even if just some of the time.

Chapter 7: Provide Them Safe Spaces. After reading thousands of employee engagement survey comments, I've concluded that employees don't always feel safe to express their true thoughts, ideas that might be counter to the mainstream, or things that make them feel uncomfortable for fear of some type of attack or retribution. The caring leader makes sure to create spaces free of judgment in which to have conversations where employees can feel psychologically safe and be free from microaggressions.

Chapter 8: Empower Them to Make Decisions. One of the most crippling things managers do to those they lead is micromanage their every move, making it difficult for their employees to think and act independently. The caring leader trades micromanagement for clear expectations and empowerment, by allowing room for employees to do what they think is right even if that means making a mistake. Such mistakes are seen as learning and growth opportunities. These leaders understand that true growth and learning comes through empowerment via clear guidance and that those they lead are adults who can make their own decisions.

Chapter 9: Build Their Resilience. Inside and outside the workplace, obstacles and challenges are all around. The caring leader focuses on building resilience within those he leads to help them respond to inevitable adversity and bounce back to become stronger. This involves helping them reframe their current circumstances, learn from what is happening around them, and see the challenges and obstacles in their paths as opportunities to grow and progress in their careers.

Chapter 10: The ROI of Caring Leadership. There is an ongoing debate regarding whether heart-based, caring leadership leads to hard-core business results such as greater revenues, greater customer satisfaction, and increased productivity. This chapter provides direct correlations between these business metrics and what some consider, as I described above, the soft skills.

Most people spend the majority of their waking hours at work. What they experience and feel while they walk around the halls of their workplaces or interact virtually exponentially impacts how they feel about themselves; how they treat their families; whether they volunteer in their communities; when and if they take vacations; and whether they live healthy, thriving lives.

By highlighting nine of the most common behaviors of caring leaders, I hope to change the minds and behaviors of leaders around the world and, by extension, uplift teams and organizations everywhere! Will you join me?

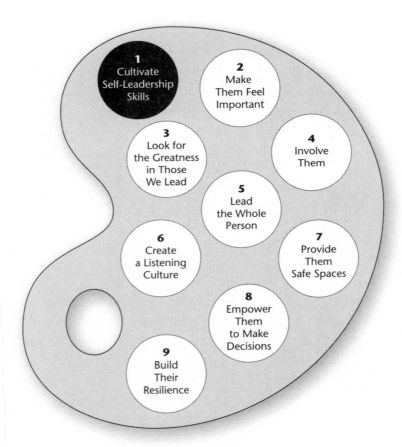

The Caring Leadership Framework

1

Cultivate Self-Leadership Skills

• • •

*The most powerful leadership tool you
have is your own personal example.*
John Wooden

Self-leadership is of critical importance for the caring leader, in that if she doesn't lead herself first, she cannot properly care for those she leads. She must understand her purpose and why she leads; be self-aware and understand and adapt to the people around her; have control over her mindset; understand the role of influence; consistently grow her skills; have a coach or mentor; and simply take time to care for her mind, body, and spirit.

Understanding the "Why" for Leading

Simon Sinek popularized this concept of knowing or finding your "why" in his 2009 book, *Start With Why*.[1] What did Sinek mean by "why"? He explains, "When I say WHY, I don't mean to make money—that's a result. By WHY I mean what is your purpose, cause, or belief? WHY does your company exist? WHY do you get out of bed every morning? And WHY should anyone care?"

In my interviews with every leader I speak with on my podcast, I often ask them where their drive to lead comes from. This is just my way of asking them about their "why" for leading. Their answer to this question really does set the tone for everything else they tell me. I do not mean to imply that once they know their drive to lead, they will be perfect leaders. Rhoda Banks, vice president, head of talent management at Rabo AgriFinance, said it perfectly: "I am really big on figuring out what our purpose is in life and living it out loud. So, if you believe that your purpose is to influence and impact others in a positive way through leadership, what better way to be able to do that? Then, every decision you make, every action you take, everything you do should be aligned with that purpose."

During our interview, Phil Cohen, founder and president of Cohen Architectural Woodworking, summed it up this way: "There's only one thing you need to remember if you want to work at a place—find out why the owner is in business, or wherever you go, find out why the leader is there, find out why he's in business. The leader's heart will tell you everything about what it's like to work there." The same holds true whether you own a business or lead a small or large team or organization. It is, indeed, the leader's heart and how he expresses it to those he leads that tells us whether he genuinely cares.

Below is a sprinkling of responses from leaders on my podcast when asked about their drive to lead. All provide insight into the heart and mind of the caring leader:

> My inspiration is, I do feel like I'm put here for a purpose and very in touch with the fact that there's just some God-given thing that I'm here to fulfill for this world, and I have a responsibility to do it. And part of that, I know, has to do with helping people to be their best selves. And I feel that we spend so much time in our workplace. Why not have our best selves show up there? **—Judith Scimone, senior VP, chief talent officer, MetLife**

> I want to be a servant-oriented leader. When I really dug deep into this idea of loving and serving, it's coming every day and . . . trying to figure out how do I serve the people that report to me so that they can be successful? How do I enable them to be successful? How do I help them grow? . . . How do I correct along the way? **—Daniel McCollum, founder and CEO, Torrent Consulting**

My drive to lead started during my freshman year in college. I was immediately indoctrinated into the military, where I understood the gravity of the service that I was about to enter. After I graduated, I fully understood that I was going to lead men and women, and sons and daughters, the most precious gifts that parents could give to the country. It was a pretty tremendous responsibility. **—Don Davis, county manager, Jefferson County, Colorado**

And I think my "why" is just thinking back on being a blind child and talking to parents who are like my parents. They had never met a blind person before they have a child who's blind. They don't know where to go or are scared. They don't know what the future can hold. And I talked to parents all the time. And they asked me, . . . "What does the future hold for my child?" I say, "I can't, at this point in time, honestly say it's not going to be a struggle. You're going to have to do everything right. You're going to have to fortunately live in the right school district that has the right resources. You're going to have to go above and beyond all the time to put your child in a position to live the life they want to live, and it's very hit or miss if you happen to be born into a family that has resources and has advocacy skills, and you know you can make it. If you're not, then it gets very, very hard for people." So, I would really like to be able to sit across the table from those parents and say, "No, your kid can do whatever they want to do in life. Here's how, here are the resources. Here are the pathways. Here are some examples." **—Kirk Adams, president and CEO, American Foundation for the Blind**

Given the fact that I've been so fortunate in my life, the one thing that drives me every single day is to make my parents proud and just to show that all their sacrifice and trust in me and faith in me is paying off. And I'm doing that by contributing back to the state that I live in and into my community. **—Patty Salazar, executive director, Colorado Department of Regulatory Agencies**

Many of the leaders I interviewed were driven to lead by personal adversity, by exposure to wonderful leaders inside and outside of their home, and through a deep calling to do something good in the world. No matter the reason, all were clear about their "why," which helped them in their leadership journey.

My "why" stems from my own childhood (more on this in chapter 9) and culminates in a workplace experience that left me feeling that I had to be the leader who helped others care more. I, like many at work, was growing apathetic, angry, and hopeless. I worked at a place that was going through a merger of multiple companies. I tried hard to uplift those around me, but the overall culture of mistrust was growing and taking its toll on me. The leaders in charge of the merger did not properly and consistently communicate to the front line what was going on. Employees were frightened of losing their jobs. New employees who joined the company had titles that were very similar to current employees'. Heck, I found out that another employee was given my job and that I had been moved to a new role by reading about it on an intranet post!

Employees on my immediate team and those in the larger organization started to report cultural discontent. I knew someone had to try to do something to make it better. I went to the head of human resources in the Denver office and said, "We have got to do something about our engagement and all the mistrust!" She replied, "You are right! You should go do something about that. You are the perfect person for that." I was shocked at this response, because I was leading customer experience at the time. After some reflection, though, I realized that there was truth to it. Before this conversation, I had begun to feel myself fall into a pit of despair. I knew that I already served as a sort of culture-bearer. I seized the opportunity to be the change I was seeking.

So, I convened an employee engagement council that had employees from many of the companies involved in the merger as its members. We curated opportunities for everyone to connect and build trust. In short order, we could see trust grow between people because we put them into situations where they had to learn more about one another, the similarities and the differences. It was a beautiful sight. Nonetheless, the merger itself did not go well, and they laid off a few hundred people. I was one. That layoff put me on the path I am on now.

Along with my childhood journey, that layoff made me realize that I was supposed to be the voice for those who could not speak for themselves or who did not have a seat at the decision-making table. I needed to be the bridge for increased enlightenment. My "why" drives me to show deep concern and kindness to others in consistent ways.

Being Congruent

To lead with a caring heart, leaders must be congruent in who they want to be and who they actually are, both out in the world and behind closed doors. All leaders are in a constant battle to create more alignment or congruence in how they show up to those they lead and how they want to show up.

The beloved Howard Behar, former president of Starbucks and a member of the *Leadership With Heart* podcast community, shared an example of what this battle looks like when he described an exchange he had with his wife of forty years, who is an oncology social worker. Howard is a well-known author and leader. He was continually trying to push his wife to be a writer because she was good at it, but she did not have a desire to write. It did not speak to her soul as it does to Howard's. It was more about his dream and the thing that drives him and not what drives her. One night, they were at dinner and they got into an argument because Howard mentioned the writing thing again. He slept on the couch that night, and he woke up early in the morning and apologized to her for thinking about himself and not about what she wanted.

Here is what Howard said in reflection: "One of my mission statements for myself goes like this: 'Every day, I want to nurture and inspire the human spirit. Beginning with myself first and then for others.' I say 'self' first, because what I've learned after living this long is if I'm not OK with Howard, then I can't help anybody else." Howard did not feel, in this example, that he was nurturing and inspiring his wife's human spirit by forcing the issue of writing with her. By extension, he did not feel congruent with his personal mission. His willingness to self-correct and admit his mistakes is a key behavior of a caring leader.

Howard's reflection brings up for me how hard it is to be congruent in all parts of our lives. I am a mother of four children. I am also certified in emotional and social intelligence and in communication styles. You would think I would be the master of congruence if you assumed that I am self-aware at all times. This is not always the case. I might find myself writing a post on social media or sending an email about being a more compassionate communicator and then turn around and yell at my kids when they need me to sit and listen. I see myself as a compassionate communicator, but I do not always show up that way. Like many other leaders, I battle to be congruent. It is a fight worth fighting if we are to be effective at caring for those we lead.

It boils down to what Daniel McCollum, founder and CEO of Torrent Consulting, said during our interview: "I came to a realization that if I'm going to get up and talk about growing leaders and being servant oriented and growing and developing, I, as the CEO, have to be the one that grows the fastest, leads the most—that serves the most of anybody in the company. So, if I can't keep up and I can't model that, then nobody else will be able to."

As both Howard and Daniel allude, being congruent also requires a greater self-awareness and a deep desire to show up true to one's self. It also requires intentionality. Personally, I remain more congruent when at the end of each day I examine what happened and whether I showed up as I intended and in line with my personal values.

Be Intentional

As leaders, we must understand one truth: People are always watching us. They are paying attention to our actions, our words, and what we fail to say. There is no getting past this. We must be intentional about what they see and hear. We can choose to control this. This might mean that we exercise good emotional self-management when in meetings or sitting with team members. We may work hard to maintain a positive, forward-thinking mindset or simply set a plan and then stick to it.

None of what I have written in this book happens by accident. We must be purposeful and aware of who we are, recognize our perceived gaps, and go about filling those gaps. Our desire to be a caring leader is an evolutionary process. We will make mistakes that can be painful, but they serve as exciting opportunities to learn. Through our intentionality to change and improve for ourselves, we earn the right to stay on the journey to caring leadership. If we do not set our intent from the start, our entire journey will feel like an accident. We will feel that we control less.

Carey Jenkins, CEO of Substantial, a digital strategy firm, described her focus on intentionality around her mindset and the conversations she has with those she leads: "I am incredibly intentional with the conversations I have about the way I support and mentor people and my expectations for what we are trying to do at the company and how people contribute to that." For Carey, intentional looks like being very clear about expectations and how others can contribute their gifts to the mission. She is a direct communicator who does not leave others guessing.

Ron Alvesteffer, CEO of Service Express, recalled for me a time when he was not the caring leader he is today and what he intentionally did to change:

> I led with the relationship with my team first and started with "Hey, how are you doing? What are the roadblocks? What do you need from me?" instead of "Go do this for me." Go solve their problems and go to work for them. Before a meeting, I would be purposeful; I would make sure I am leading the person sitting before me first. We will get to the numbers later. You have to be purposeful or it can get away from you, and now you are talking about numbers and business results. It's the people who deliver the numbers and business results. When you get that in the wrong order, it doesn't work out well. A great culture and focusing on the people will deliver the results.

I still remember my conversation with Ron and how he was clear about his intentional change of mind and how he treated his people. It was as if he had become awakened to the fact that he held the brush and could choose his own brushstrokes in demonstrating care for his people.

Christinne Johnson, president of human resources at FirstBank, reflected with me on a time when she went into a meeting prepared to present a big change she was going to be leading. She admitted that when she had met resistance, she let her ego get in the way and felt triggered and was very emotional. Christinne even planned for a colleague to signal her when she was crossing any lines, but she ignored her colleague's signals. After the meeting, she took a time-out to reflect on the situation, realized that she should have been more in control of her emotions, and decided that she had to make things right. She gathered her thoughts and then took time to meet individually with different people who had been at the meeting and apologize to them. Regarding that interaction, she said, "That was really defining for me, because I really do try more now to have that . . . pause in the situation when I know that something is starting to trigger me a little bit and just pause because I am very passionate."

Leaders set the tone for their teams and organizations. Period. If we do not own that truth, we can never uplift those we lead. Adding another level of texture to the importance of being intentional, Keith Freier, director of operational systems and technology at Pacific Northwest National Laboratory, so simply added this when reflecting on the movie *Remember the Titans*: "It gets back to that attitude reflects leadership again. . . . You have to set that positive tone; the organization is going to follow with that tone. If you come in grumpy and kicking the walls, guess what the rest of the organization is going to do? The same thing. So, that's something that I've always tried to . . . keep whatever's burdening me at home."

Keith is so right! I loved *Remember the Titans* exactly for the reason Keith referenced. The main character, as portrayed by Denzel Washington, acts with great intention and conviction by setting aside the tough racial climate of segregation in the 1960s and choosing to lead and grow his team's unity. In short, intentionality requires focus.

As Washington's character made clear, intentionality requires that leaders set their minds right in advance of interactions, especially when they know they might experience conflict or conflicting views. Megan Bertrand, senior vice president of learning and development at FirstBank, takes this concept home for us in a powerful way: "You're never going to change how others react and say things. You're never going to change those persons. But you, as yourself, can change how you react to them and to the situation."

Megan confessed that prior to holding that belief, she was struggling in her professional relationships, especially with those who had different personalities and ways of thinking than hers. She admitted wanting to change those people, but she realized quickly that she needed to change her reaction to them and her mindset. She realized that she needed to hold up a mirror to herself and be purposeful in changing.

Since I was very young, I have worked hard to be intentional in my thinking and in how I relate to others. I find that I do this by focusing forward and using my mission and vision like a sort of bull's-eye. Then, I load action up front aligned with that mission that keeps me focused and without much time to look back or get stuck.

As stated in the introduction, anyone seeking to become a caring leader must first have an awareness that they need to change and a desire to do the work required to change. So many leaders out in the world think of themselves as caring leaders, but the recipients of that type of leadership are the gauge of whether caring leadership behaviors are exhibited. It is worthwhile to be intentional. It is the only way to become a caring leader. During my leader interviews, none of them recalled a time of successful leadership that did not include being purposeful and reflective.

Have a Support System

I can attest to the fact that leaders cannot do it alone. They need to have a support system in place, whether it be close colleagues, friends, mentors, or coaches. Any leader who tries to lead people without at least occasionally seeking counsel cannot be a caring leader. Why? Hindsight is never as clear as we'd like it to be. When we enlist the help of others, we gain more foresight and develop strategies to bypass possible barriers in our way.

Phil Burgess, chief people and operations officer at C Space, clearly understands why having a support system is critical. When Phil needs a "safe space to be a vulnerable leader," he turns to other leaders who are going through the same thing, with whom he can talk about all the stuff that might be going wrong. He chooses to lean on them for good counsel.

On the same concept of finding people you can trust to provide honest feedback and ensure that you are on the path you intend, Cori Burbach, assistant city manager for the City of Dubuque, Iowa, shared that she, too, leans on colleagues across the country whom she trusts and to whom she can say, "Here's what I'm trying. I'm stuck." And they can say, "Oh, Cory, remember this about yourself? That's why you're reacting this way. What if you looked at it this way instead?"

Keith Freier, the leader I mentioned in the "Be Intentional" section above, elevated this concept by introducing the idea of having a "personal board of directors." Keith realized that there is power in selecting more than one mentor. In fact, he discovered that not all leaders shine in every area. He uncovered the fact that he could increase his effectiveness if he could emulate the strengths of many different mentors.

I especially love this idea, because I have found that people get so busy, and it can be hard to find time to confer if you and they are in meetings frequently. Nonetheless, almost anyone who is close to you would be willing to give one hour per quarter! Phil, Cory, and Keith all realized that they needed a support system that was a little less formal than hiring a coach to help them stay centered and clear.

Taking it a step further, some of my *Leadership With Heart* guests mentioned that they did hire a coach to help them sort things out regarding their leadership, communication, organizational management, and much more. As an executive coach myself, I know that being a more formal sounding board to leaders who have the power to impact the experience for so many in the workplace is priceless. I can provide a third-party, educated view on complicated topics.

Mike Pritchard, chief financial officer at Volunteers of America Colorado, highly recommends consulting with a coach. "I just think it's hard to do it alone. I do think the benefit of a one-on-one coach really will help somebody just get centered on where they are, and this coach hopefully can help you explore what you need to do to be a better leader."

This is exactly what happened with Rich Todd, principal and CEO of Innovest Portfolio Solutions. Rich went from a place filled with ego and caring mostly about the survival of his firm to a place where culture and employees came first. Rich and his partners decided to hire a CEO coach who advised them to shift the firm's focus away from him as the founder and more toward a culture of empowerment. They started taking small steps to include people and recognize them. Now, they direct substantial resources toward social responsibility and volunteering as a company in the community, leadership development, and professional development.

Of that long-term coaching relationship, Rich reflected, "Taking the firm in a different direction, it made me a lot better person, and I'm in it, and we've grown immensely since then. And it has little to do with me. It has a lot more to do with others that are here. It's a great life lesson."

I have not had formal mentors in my life, but I have called on coaches, close friends, and family when I needed to see things in a different light. I am a predominantly self-reliant person who is very much mission driven, but even I have placed the occasional frantic call to a colleague who I know understands me and will think more clearly than I am able at that moment.

This is also part of my "why" for being an executive coach for leaders who need help with interpersonal skills and relationships. I want to be their sounding board, their safe place where they can bring anything with which they are struggling. Leaders who do what Phil, Cori, Mike, and Rich did by committing to create a support system, whether informal or formal, to use as a sounding board for their leadership can begin to leave traces of caring leadership on the hearts of those they lead. Another important element to focus on is exercising self-care.

Exercise Self-Care

We hear a lot about self-care. As a mother of four children, I could not survive, let alone thrive, as a parent without it. Moreover, as a longtime compassionate leader of teams, I remember when my own self-care fell short, and so did my ability to lead those teams well.

What do I mean by self-care? In the simplest sense, it is taking care of ourselves. We cannot effectively show care for others until we give ourselves the same courtesies.

I love how Alex Smith, chief human resources officer and chief change officer for the City of Memphis, framed this issue so clearly: "You've got to put the oxygen mask on yourself first before you can put it on other people. I do believe that it is really important. Otherwise, you can end up putting yourself in a position where you can't help anyone, because you're ill or you're not in the best capacity to do so."

Striving to become a more caring leader is a complex concept. While we want to be more focused on those who look to us for care and guidance, we must also take close care of ourselves. A significant part of this is what Christinne Johnson of FirstBank described as "having grace for ourselves." She explained, "We, as individuals, especially those who are in leadership, because we are high achievers and high performers striving forward, we have a tendency to want to be perfect all the time, be perceived as being perfect, and will give grace to others." Christine added that "caring for ourselves also models that behavior" for those who look to us for guidance. Our expression of self-care then gives them permission to do the same for themselves.

Some examples of self-care might be establishing a workout routine every morning to clear our minds, having a regular appointment with a mental health professional to talk through recurring issues that need focus, spending time in prayer and meditation, taking a group yoga class, or even sitting down with a financial adviser to plan our future, to name a few. We all know what fills us up and makes us feel energized to take on the day and show up as our best selves. Personally, I work out in some form every morning, usually before my four kids awaken. It's my time for calm and quiet.

As Christinne was quoted above, self-care is also giving ourselves the freedom to be imperfect. In other words, we need to exercise self-compassion. Self-compassion, which was put into practice by Kristin Neff, associate professor of human development and culture, Educational Psychology Department, University of Texas at Austin, "involves acting the same way towards yourself [as you do toward others] when you are having a difficult time, fail, or notice something you don't like about yourself. Instead of just ignoring your pain with a 'stiff upper lip' mentality, you stop to tell yourself, 'This is really difficult right now; how can I comfort and care for myself in this moment?'"[2]

When we exercise self-compassion, then, we rest into the truth that our mistakes do not define us as people. We don't allow our mishaps to reign over our minds. We care for ourselves, which allows us to fully care for those we lead. I know that this can be easier said than done, but with support and a consistent focus on caring for our mind, body, soul, and spirit, we can get there.

Just as an artist has many instruments to create beautiful works of art, so too must leaders care for every aspect of themselves to deliver their own unique leadership. Self-care is really one of the greatest instruments that leaders can access to deliver beautiful experiences for those they lead. It is also one of the greatest gifts we give those around us. An additional critical behavior on which to focus is being authentically you.

Be Authentically You

"I think one of the most important things is to know yourself. People see authenticity, and they know it right away when they see it, and they'll get behind that." I absolutely love this simple quote from Jim Reuter, president and CEO of FirstBank! If I want to be a caring leader, I must be authentically me.

What does authenticity look like in the context of the caring leader? It means that we do not show up one way for one person or group and another way for someone else. We are who we are, no matter what, and we do not pretend to be someone that we are not. We do not shy away from telling the truth about ourselves. In fact, we endear ourselves to others because of that truth.

To be authentically me, I must know myself well. Otherwise, my behaviors might shift in the wind. To know myself well means that I am self-aware of what might trigger me, what makes me smile, what makes me react or be proactive.

I choose every day to show up authentically me. I know that I am successful in this because this is how others describe me. Leaders who shy away from being authentic either don't know themselves well or are afraid of how others might think of them. I spent a lot of my life not feeling good enough or worthy to be fully me.

I do not think I arrived at "me" until my early thirties. This was after I realized that I was trying to be someone else to meet my family's expectations of me. Once I let that go, I was free to show up as fully me. That allowed me to be fully present and care more deeply for those who looked to me for guidance. Before that, I was just a shell of the real me.

Megan Smiley Wick, executive director of Gamma Phi Beta Sorority and Foundation, highlighted the importance of not only knowing one-self but also being able to manage oneself. She explained, "I know a lot about myself, but being able to recognize those things in the moment and manage them has been a . . . very long journey." Megan recognized that over her leadership journey, whenever she lost the ability to manage her emotions, she was not the best leader.

One example Megan shared was when she was in a group meeting and felt threatened or questioned by someone there. She described how she would respond in that situation: "I move too quickly, I become im-patient, I become less sensitive or become too direct, and then I begin to erode trust." Megan worked with a coach and took some assessments to help her land on ways to exercise better self-management.

I heard the sentiment that Megan expressed many times in my inter-views. The caring leaders I interviewed were all more aware of their be-haviors than the average leader I had encountered, and out of sheer desire and openness they were better able to manage their emotions and adapt.

Dirk Frese, vice president of sales, marketing, and service at Julabo USA, pointed to the fact that a leader's level of authenticity is directly correlated to how freely others want to follow her: "We have to be cou-rageous enough to open up ourselves to our employees, that they can see us . . . that they can see our personality. We have to share our personal stories with them. We are not . . . robots. We are human beings. . . . Then they follow us in a highly motivated way."

Remember, though, being authentic also means that none of us are perfect, but we are uniquely who we are. Being authentic also means that we don't always show up as the best version of ourselves. As Dirk pointed out, we are all human. As such, we must work hard to reveal the best of ourselves. This effort is part of the daily actions we must focus on if we are to become the caring leaders our people need us to be.

Kristi Turner, chief marketing officer at Compeat Restaurant Management Software, used powerful descriptors to describe this: "Show up in every moment right with that powerful blend of authenticity, humility, self-confidence. And when you do that, . . . each individual will create a kind of tsunami of power that ignites good . . . in the world and everybody around you, and that's what makes you a great leader."

As I listened to Kristi, Dirk, Megan, and Jim using these powerful words, I was inspired to live in my own shoes and show up as my best self and help others do the same. The idea of caring leadership as more art than science came alive in these exchanges.

Another important point here is that authenticity means we will show up differently, look differently, speak differently, see things differently. This also represents our authentic selves. Those we lead are a diverse set of people, as are we. When they see that we are being true to who we are, they will do the same and feel cared for as a result. Another ingredient in showing up as a caring leader is to own your own growth.

Own Your Own Growth

Being a manager is tough. Not only do we have to manage the day-to-day tasks and meet timelines and complete projects, but also we are expected to grow people and keep them happy. Often, I say that leadership is a journey, not a destination. We do not ever "arrive" to being the perfect caring leader, but we do have to work every day to be better, to grow ourselves and learn.

Early on in my leadership journey, I worked as an independent consultant for Mary Kay, the cosmetics company. It was the best investment in my leadership skills, as they taught me so much about building relationships with my team members. Whenever there was a conference or training opportunity, I would show up with enthusiasm, because I was so happy to have the opportunity to learn and grow. I grew a lot in the role and grew my team as a result.

During my interview with Rich Gassen, printing production manager at the University of Wisconsin–Madison, he exhibited a hunger for knowledge and learning new ways to motivate his team. Nonetheless, as he recalled for me, he was not always focused on these things. Rich spoke of a time early on in his management career when he inherited team members who had attendance and work ethic issues. While he was trying to establish more team building, the team was not on board, and he had to take disciplinary action. He admitted that he had not been prepared to handle any of it. So, with the help of his manager at the time, he sought out training resources to prepare him for tough situations. He confessed, "I wasn't the best leader early on, when I was kind of winging it."

It takes courage to admit that we are not perfect and then seek out the help we need. What I loved most about this exchange with Rich was his reflection on how he had not shown up as a caring leader early in his management career but refocused his efforts to change by seeking personal training and development. Rich exhibited self-awareness, and then he used it to grow himself so that he could lead more effectively.

Just as Rich made some changes to grow himself because of challenges in the workplace, Trent Selbrede, a general manager at Marriott International, did the same thing after realizing that he was "bored, irritable, and stopped having fun in life." Trent admitted having an interaction with a team member that ended in that team member leaving the company the very next day. In response, Trent focused on owning his own growth and enrolled in a master's hospitality program. He invested in funding his education because he was "determined to change" himself.

Within a few months of starting the program, he could see the transformation take hold. It helped him change others' perceptions of him because he was more self-aware, which helped him become a better leader. He shared, "I think that it really helped me figure out I need to be a better father, I need to be a better leader at work, I need to be a better husband, I need to do better at a lot of things."

I listened to many leadership growth stories like those above, and I was inspired each time by the individual's struggle to get better. That is what I am inviting us all to do: just get a little better every day. By doing so, we are better able to express more care for those we lead.

The Art of Caring Leadership in Practice

It is just not possible to sustain caring leadership without doing the inner work to get there. Block off time on your calendar now to take time for you. Consider journaling how you are feeling daily, and reflect on it with a coach or close colleague. Stand in front of a mirror and evaluate if you like what you see and if you are doing work that lights your soul on fire.

Caring Leader Highlight

Karen Johnson
equity and inclusion administrator
Washington Department of Corrections

Interviewed on: Episode 106, "Leaders with Heart Are Human and Give Others Permission to Be the Same"

- **Industry/specialization:** Public safety (corrections)

- **Aha moment:** As the staff assistant to the director at the Cleveland VA Medical Center, Karen was tasked with healing the racial divide between staff and veteran patients, managing a $3 million design project, and overseeing the Equal Employment Opportunity office. A strictly results-oriented leader, Karen said she was hyper-focused on her duties, often at the expense of caring for those around her. "At one point, the staff I was supervising basically called me every word under the sun and told me how horrible I was as their boss," Karen shared. "So, I was sent home for the month of October to just rest from all the work that I had put in. And at that time, I was thinking about what my staff had said. I reflected on what they told me that was true, and virtually all that was true." Heeding her peers' feedback, Karen became committed to cultivating her self-leadership skills so that she could better lead others. After returning to her faith-based practice, spending time searching for her joy and happiness, and tending to her own emotional garden, Karen came out the other side of her professional crisis a better leader and a better person.

- **How they embody caring leadership:** This chapter is focused on cultivating self-leadership skills if we hope to lead others. Karen demonstrates exactly why leadership starts within: "I wasn't really loving myself properly, and therefore I did not have the capacity to love others adequately. . . . And so that really, really changed the trajectory for my leadership philosophy, and I'm to this day thankful for those individuals for speaking truth to me." In order to gain her staff's trust and faith, she had to question her own motivations and communication style and recalibrate her inner belief system.

- **Guiding philosophy:**

  - *Lead yourself; then lead others; and finally, lead together.* Karen believes we need to show our humanity to others at work, so they feel empowered to do the same. She said, "What's going on with us impacts what's going on with the team. And if we don't have self-awareness or we don't have the capacity to self-reflect and grow and course-correct, well, that does not give anybody else permission to do the same." Once we feel safe enough to bring our entire selves to work, we can leverage the strengths and assets of that new and more holistic workforce.

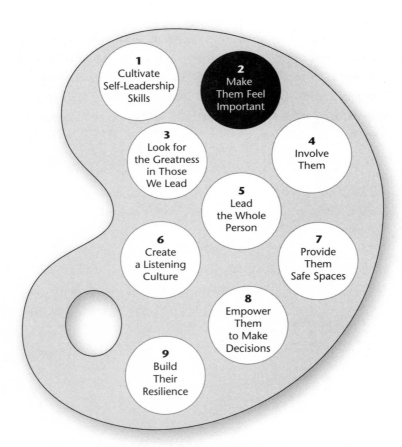

The Caring Leadership Framework

2

• • •

Make Them Feel Important

Showing your team members that you want to know them as people and not just as a number on a payroll list helps them to feel important and valued. Then, they turn around and do it for your customers!
Denise Testori, president and CEO, Prestige Cleaners

Many employees don't feel seen by those who are supposed to lead them. They often feel like a number. The caring leader makes sure to set time with her people one-on-one and listens intently to what her employees need from her to do their best work. When this type of leader is around, employees feel like they are the only ones who matter. Employees feel a deep connection with this type of leader because they feel that they can be their best selves and they are appreciated for the work they put in.

As I described in the previous chapter, I learned a lot about leadership working for Mary Kay. Mary Kay Ash herself was a caring leader. One of the things she believed in was that no matter if there were fifty women lined up to speak with her, the person in front of her was the most important in that moment. She did not let her eyes veer off that person and listened and gave the person her undivided attention. This stuck with me.

I love how Rich Todd, CEO at Innovest, summed it up: "The best way to get somebody's attention and lead them is to serve them." That is what we do when we show them sincere appreciation, get in the trenches with them, and connect with them at a deeper level. Caring leaders intentionally put this connection at the top of their list and express it often through their actions. Let's take a closer look at each of these behaviors.

Recognize Them

Author Adrian Gostick once said, "The celebration of one success launches a thousand more." This is one of the truest things about leadership. Showing sincere appreciation for those we lead makes them want to do more of the thing that produced the recognition. It also instills a sense that they are important in and of themselves.

Denise Testori, president and CEO of Prestige Cleaners, writes employees thank-you or congratulatory notes that might say, "I'm really proud of you. I know you worked really hard and this was a big goal of yours, and here you are!" Then, Denise and her team choose some type of gift card that resonates specifically with that team member and give it to him or her.

Denise highlights an extremely important point: We must find out what it is that motivates those we lead and understand what we need to do to make them feel appreciated. If we recognize someone in a way that does not suit the person, we could make him or her feel anxious and not uplifted.

Brigitte Grimm, chief deputy treasurer of Larimer County, Colorado, gets this when she asks her team members, "What motivates you?" Then, she keeps their answers in mind when interacting with them. Brigitte takes recognition to another level: "So, when we have our monthly birthday meeting, if someone's taking a class, I like them to get up and share with us some of the great things in the class that they learned or that they want to share with us. So, we really focus on giving each employee time to shine."

Many times, without our knowing, those we lead are depressed, anxious, and lonely, but when we show them appreciation, they know that they are important in our life. It is important that we be the gift bearers of recognition so they will know that we notice and value the tiniest of milestones they achieve. Believe it or not, our words of praise might be the only positive light our people receive for weeks on end.

Steve Browne, vice president of human resources at LaRosa's Pizzeria, Inc., showed his complete understanding of this concept when he shared, "I don't think that we affirm people enough to say that what they do matters. We tend to rank it or put something above another thing. Without our team members, I don't have a job. I think just reminding people that the contribution they have matters."

Farouk Rajab, general manager at Marriott International, simply stated, "Let's start with a thank-you, because you know how hard they worked. You have to recognize how hard they've worked, and you have to recognize that it was a busy time for them."

I recall taking part in my first 360 feedback assessment. A few colleagues commented that they did not understand how I had so much time to recognize so many people in the organization when I would send emails. My colleagues thought I could spend my time in other ways. What they did not comprehend was that I knew what it felt like to feel less important. In many ways, when I was growing up, I was withering on the vine for feeling less than. As a result, I refused to be the person who made others feel that their efforts were inconsequential. To the contrary, I wanted people to know that I noticed their contributions. Could I be putting my effort elsewhere? Yes, but I made it a top priority to show sincere appreciation to those around me.

Denise, Brigitte, Steve, and Farouk all made clear the importance of showing genuine appreciation for those we lead. In a sense, they saw their expression of this behavior as the defining characteristic of their leadership.

Caring leaders also take advantage of formal communication channels within their organizations to recognize employees. A picture on a website, a social media shout-out, or a mention in a newsletter means a lot, as it gives us an opportunity to be seen by friends and family. These kinds of recognition are bound to further good will and strengthen the bonds between caring leaders and those they lead.

By expressing genuine appreciation consistently, we are taking daily actions to show concern and kindness for those we lead. This makes their desire to stay on our team stronger. Another way to create a sense of importance in those we lead is to get in the trenches with them.

Get in the Trenches

Some years ago, I facilitated a culture team made up of frontline employees. One of its members, in an attempt to highlight a disconnect between the senior team and the plight of the front line, said, "When the bigwigs come out to where we work, make sure they don't do it on a bright and sunny day, but on a rainy and sloppy day. That way, they can experience what we experience, and they can get their shoes dirty."

Through my work listening to employees, I've perceived that many feel a disconnect between their struggles, wants, and desires and what the senior team understands about the front line. One of the things I uncovered during the process of interviewing leaders was that many mentioned getting in the trenches with their people, even occasionally.

I absolutely loved how Eric Jacobsen, COO at Kalnin Ventures, referred to this when discussing ways to stay connected to his people. He shared his philosophy, learned from a previous manager: "Do you want to catch fish? You have to cast among them." Eric recommended that we "cast among" our people by popping in to see them, dropping by the coffee bar, mixing with them while they are working or brainstorming.

Cori Burbach of the City of Dubuque literally got in the trenches with her people when she did some flood recovery work with groups of volunteers. She kept a picture of herself taken with some of the volunteers. She was wearing a breathing mask and was covered in black muck. Of that experience she said, "But that picture to me, I hope that's how people see me. That I'm willing to roll up my sleeves and get the work done alongside the people, whatever we need to do to make an impact."

Rich Gassen recalled a time when he and other frontline employees worked to solve a problem until 2 a.m., and his manager stayed with him the entire time, and they solved the problem together. Of that experience, Rich recalled, "He had my back, and he was there with me the whole time. I imported that into my leadership style."

Keith Freier said it beautifully: "I'm really kind of that roll-up-the-sleeves kind of guy. . . . I'm not going to ask them to do something I wouldn't be willing to do myself."

Eric, Rich, Cori, and Keith's mindsets and behaviors are the hallmarks of a caring leader. Leaders who add their own special contributions to the team endear them to those around them. They uplift teams and organizations simply by their willingness to dig in and show up. They also do this by connecting deeply with each team member.

Connect Deeply

I love this quote by Dirk Frese of Julabo USA, when he spoke about the power of connection: "Sometimes you cannot look each other in the eyes, but if you listen to the heart of the other person, then you can connect, and when you connect, you can empower your staff or you can empower your customer, and motivate him or her."

Connection can sound like a deep and elusive concept, but the leaders I interviewed innately understood how important it is to connect with those we lead and in turn bolster their trust. Joe Kwon, associate director of the Global Privacy and Information Management Office at KPMG US, called connection a "universal principle" when he shared, "In order to move someone, they have to trust you. They have to connect with you, first, before you even have a chance to influence them or persuade them in a way that is ethical and beneficial for both parties."

Cynthia Grant, chief operations officer and chief clinical officer at AllHealth Network, infused even more depth when she said, "That's part of where we come from. . . . People have a universal desire to work and to live in a culture that is connected, and when we're disconnected, that's when we struggle."

Dirk, Joe, and Cynthia highlight one of the most critical focuses for the caring leader, but how do caring leaders truly connect with those they lead? First, they set aside time to spend with their team members. Second, they reveal pieces of themselves to their people. Third, they are accessible to those who look to them for guidance and support. Let's discuss each of these in more depth.

Set Aside Time to Be with Those You Lead

You might be wondering why I separated setting aside time for those we lead and being accessible to those we lead. The difference is nuanced, but they are worth discussing separately. When I refer to "setting aside time to be with them," I mean that we proactively mark time on our calendars weekly or bimonthly to sit with them. When I refer to "being accessible," I mean that we are there when they need us or come to us in a more spontaneous way. Both leave the people we lead feeling important, and both are staples for the caring leader.

I love how Mindy Flanigan, founder and chief inspiration officer of Inspiring HR, put it: "One thing I've learned, whether you're remote or you're in an office with the people that work with you every day, you've got to give everybody individual face time." This separate undivided attention helps those we lead feel truly seen and valued for just being them.

Steve Browne of LaRosa's Pizzeria showed all heart when he explained why he chooses to intentionally connect with his people: "I don't care about my desk. I care about the people. So, I will spend time with people intentionally, to hear the good stories, to hear the rough stories, and to genuinely understand how things are going."

When Tim Hinchey III, president and CEO of USA Swimming, joined the organization as CEO, he set out to meet the employees by having each one sign up to walk with him to have coffee for an hour to get to know one another. Of his intentions, he said, "I don't want to be the jerk in the corner office that thinks he knows what he's doing to lead our company. I want to have a real, authentic relationship with people. That's first and foremost."

Several years ago, one of my team members and I were conducting a candidate interview in my office. The candidate asked us, "What's so great about your team, and why should I choose it?" This was a great question, and I chose to let my team member answer it. He paused, for what seemed like thirty minutes, and said, "This lady right here! I immediately looked behind me to see who he was referring to and then said, "Me? No!" Then my team member said, "Yes, you!" He continued his explanation: "Before she came, we would rarely see a senior manager—no one really stopped by to just check on us—and you also set up time to meet with us weekly. Not everyone did that for us. She makes us feel important!"

Whew! I hadn't been quite sure what he would say. I was proud of his response because I had spent my leadership career working hard to make people feel like that. This was just the first time someone had validated my efforts in this way. I had more pep in my step for the rest of the day, and that candidate decided to join our team. He was a great addition.

Often, leaders get sidetracked by travel and being in different offices around the country. Nonetheless, there are ways to stay connected to those people, and the payoff is big on all sides. Pat Brady, regional president at FirstBank, described his thinking about focusing on personal connection: "You have got to be present still, even though you do a lot of things electronically . . . physical presence is important. I do travel to out-of-state markets often. That's a meeting protocol, but I also schedule smaller meetings with some of their people for breakfast or lunch."

Nate Igielinski, service and parts field operations manager at FCA Fiat Chrysler Automobiles, described the need to connect one-on-one with his remote team. He and his team travel a lot for work. His whole focus is having a personal relationship with them. He explained partly how he does that: "I've got to travel with them, and that means that either I go out to them, or they're coming in to me, and more likely I always go out to them." Nate works hard to see each of his team members in person and not just via emails, texts, or phone calls. It is difficult to manage a remote team, but he understands the importance of seeing one another face-to-face in strengthening relationships.

David Niu, CEO and founder of TINYpulse, got creative with connecting with his team, given his heavy travel schedule, by initiating a program called "TINYcoffee," whereby he schedules thirty-minute coffee sessions with his people. He described how he does this: "I just literally pick random people [at TINYpulse], and I don't have a preset agenda when I am talking to them. It's how I understand how they are doing, if there's anything I should know about that I don't know about. And I just keep it pretty fluid."

During the COVID-19 global pandemic, teams have been stretched to find other ways to connect. Video calls have become more prominent. As the world learned that they could connect via video, and they could also still see one another while using masks and social distancing, in-person connection was made possible again. This need to be near one another, whether six feet away or not, still remained an important part of feeling connected.

One of my favorite conversations on this topic was with Christinne Johnson of FirstBank. Christinne reflected on times when she was traveling a lot for work and away from her team and how she longed to see them. She explained that she felt "nourished" by hearing from her team on how they overcame certain challenges in creative ways despite her absence. She was proud of their resilience and their innovative thinking.

I adored my conversation with Christinne, and this idea of leaders being nourished by the connection with those they lead hit home for me. This is true not just for work, but also at home with our children.

Recently, I decided to go into my eldest son's room and just lie on his bed while he sat at his desk. I started to ask him questions about his life. Then he came over and sat on the bed as we continued to talk. He shared more with me, because I made time just for him. Additionally, I did not have an agenda but just to spend time with him. I, like, Christinne, felt nourished by my deeper connection with him. He also expressed how much he loves his time with me alone.

Setting aside one-on-one time and team time to meet with those we lead is so valuable. If we are to be known as a caring leader, we must do as the leaders I described above do in setting aside time to connect with our people in consistent ways. We also need to share pieces of ourselves with those we lead.

Share a Piece of You

Adam McCoy, director of human resources at Arrow Electronics, makes it clear that we must connect in genuine ways and share who we are. Adam explained that he shares some things about his life and chats with his team about what might be happening with their lives too. He mentioned that the wife of one of his coworkers was having a baby, and he would ask how they were doing.

Pat Brady strongly feels that leaders need to share a piece of themselves with their people. Connection goes both ways. Specifically, Pat explained that our people "appreciate us asking about them, but they have an interest in us and our life, how that plays out, and what it looks like. We can be real about that and share things openly. I think it only strengthens the bond, too."

The benefits of proactively connecting with those we lead are clear. Gustavo Tavares, country manager for Brazil at Top Employers Institute, said it perfectly: "You have to think of ways on how you can connect with your people so you can become a better leader. Otherwise, you'll be isolating yourself, and this isolation doesn't create anything else but confusion, lack of communication, and lack of trust."

Adam, Pat, and Gustavo all clearly understand that being more open and vulnerable about how we are feeling can go a long way toward making our people feel important and cared for.

However, the caring leader must strike the delicate balance between healthy sharing and oversharing without boundaries. Otherwise, if we share too much too often, we might lose the trust and faith of those who look to us for guidance.[1]

What might that look like? I must confess that this is one of my greatest areas of development as a leader. I remember having an interaction with someone on the executive leadership team that left me feeling deflated. I came back to my office, and one of my direct reports asked me how it had gone. I spent more time than I am proud to admit whining to her about the experience and how it left me feeling.

What do you think that team member was thinking? "Poor Heather, she really needs to get a grip" or "If she cannot handle this leader and this project, I don't think I can either!" By being overly vulnerable, I contributed to my team member's lack of confidence in me and in her. What I should have done was call on my self-awareness and learn to control my own emotions. Moreover, I should have shared a solution for the issue I faced to provide a path for how we could move forward.

So, even if I had still shared how the meeting went, I could have said something like, "It was a frustrating conversation. We have been tasked to do this project this way instead of that way. I am going to need your help in thinking through how we do this, OK?" If I had stopped there, that would have been honest and forward-looking at the same time.

In the end, selective vulnerability is critical to creating a deep sense of connection with those we lead. It is also a key leader behavior that, if expressed often, can leave our people feeling that we care for them—not just for what they can do for us but because we are in this together. We can also produce that feeling of concern and kindness for our people when we are accessible to them when they need us.

Be Accessible

So many managers choose to focus on things that are tactical and hold little importance to their team's success. Caring leaders make sure that they are accessible in meaningful ways to those they lead. Doing so promotes increased communication, a greater sense of safety, and employees who are ready and willing to go over and above.

Often leaders, especially the higher up they are in the organizational hierarchy, become distant and inaccessible to their people. This lack of accessibility creates a chasm between the frontline and executive leaders. Lon Southerland, managing director of biomic sciences at Seraphic Group, confirmed this point when he recalled an interaction he had had with a coworker after Lon was promoted. His coworker said, "I want to leave you with one bit of advice. Don't forget where you came from. . . . A lot of times, I see people move up the ranks, but the more distant they get from past positions, the more distant they also become to their staff. As a result, they do not become the best leaders."

Lon's colleague was onto something. Caring leadership is taking daily actions that show concern and kindness to those we lead. If we are not available to our people when they need us, we not only lack connection with them but lose the opportunity to demonstrate that concern.

I remember being mostly accessible to the teams I led, but I was not perfect at it. Often, I would be running around in between meetings, and my people were unable to access me. I could sense their frustration when we did connect, and I would make sure to clear away distractions and give them my undivided attention to help them through some problem or a question they had. The evidence of my caring leadership is strong, but I am not infallible. I continue to work on this at home too.

I truly appreciated when Tom Dietzler, director of operations at St. Peter Lutheran Church and School, shared how he tries to stay present when someone comes to his office. First, if someone walks in, he immediately closes his laptop. Second, if he is on a tight timeline and too busy to chat, he is honest with the person and schedules another time to talk.

Jim Reuter, FirstBank's president and CEO, acknowledged that he is consistently working on being more accessible to his team after having received direct employee feedback saying that he had removed himself in his new role as CEO. Now, what does Jim do to ensure that he stays accessible? He shared, "When I go down . . . to the café or drop something off in the mailroom, I don't have my executive assistant do it, I go do it, and I take a different path every time . . . and I run into employees in the hallway, or I swing by their workstation and check in."

Claude Silver, chief heart officer of VaynerMedia, calls this type of accessibility "holding space" for those she leads. Claude explained, "I'm here to hold space, to be of service, and to take action. That's really important to me." One way that Claude does this is to check in on new employees and have an open-door policy to see how they are doing.

Zig Ziglar, a well-known speaker and author, understood how being accessible, even to those he had never met, could create a lifelong connection and a feeling of importance. Steve Paul, principal consultant at

Six68 and former president of SPCS, happily recalled a time when he met Zig at an event. Steve was blown away by Zig's openness to make him feel important and worthy. Steve fondly remembered how Zig invited him to sit with Zig and his wife, and then Zig made Steve "the center of conversation for the next twenty minutes. . . . He kept encouraging me. I was telling him, 'You know, I feel like I don't deserve to be onstage. I need to accomplish something.' And he just wouldn't have any of it. So, I've never forgotten that." Steve said the way that Zig was accessible and made him feel important became a big part of Steve's own leadership style.

Tom, Jim, Claude, and Zig obviously got that being open and accessible to those who looked to them for guidance made their people feel important. By demonstrating actions and not just words, these leaders made those they led feel cared for.

Caring leaders understand that they must care for their people before expecting anything in return. One of the most important things you can do for any human being is to make him or her feel important. This is the sincerest form of care. When leaders recognize their people, get in the trenches with them, and connect with them deeply, they elicit such positive emotions in their people and make those they lead want to go over and above and stay with those leaders longer.

The Art of Caring Leadership in Practice

There is no higher form of care than to make someone feel important. As a leader, you can be the greatest source of positive emotions in those you lead by recognizing their efforts in specific ways, taking time to connect one-on-one, and just being there for them. Be consistent in your efforts. Choose to be the light in their lives.

Caring Leader Highlight

Erik Van Bramer
senior vice president, Federal Reserve Bank of Chicago

Interviewed on: Episode 116, "Leaders with Heart Have Care as Their North Star"

- **Industry/specialization:** Banking and finance (customer relations and support)

- **Aha moment:** Like many others, Erik had been defining his leadership style and his career path around achieving the next level. Whatever position was higher or more senior was always the goal, which drove him to great professional heights—but not without a significant cost. "I had a point in my career where I wasn't empathetic to my peers. When I got to a higher position, I forgot to think how it affected them and became more focused on myself and how wonderful this got for me," he said. "I was not thinking of the people who helped get me here." By prioritizing his professional success over the heart and soul of his job, Erik had pushed his peers aside and made them feel unimportant. What was the tipping point? "It almost took a slap in the face to see that I needed to refocus and look back at why I wanted to be here in the first place. Someone who I'd been really close to called me out and said, 'Oh sorry, Mr. Big Shot now. Why don't you tell us peons what it is we need to do next?'" Though it took a moment of brute honesty to shake Erik awake, it ultimately made him realize how poorly he was treating his team members. He eventually realized that his own success is inextricably connected to the success of his employees, and they must feel valued if he expects them to help him achieve his goals.

- **How they embody caring leadership:** This chapter explores the basic need for employees to feel important, and Erik is a beautiful example of what happens when that need isn't adequately met. He also models what a caring leader should do when faced with tough feedback:

be receptive, listen with an open mind, and respond with gratitude. Erik now looks elsewhere for motivation rather than the perpetual next level. He advised, "When you're looking for motivation, look to others as your gauge rather than to yourself."

- **Guiding philosophy:**
  - *The success of your team is your own success, and vice versa.* The hallmark of effective caring leadership is a cohesive, loyal team that works toward a common goal and activates through their hearts rather than their heads. Good leaders know that when one of their team members shines, they all shine. As Erik put it, "If I can keep the spark and enthusiasm going with everyone on my team, it sets us all up to be successful."

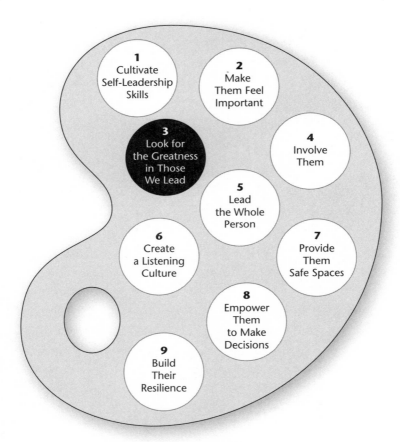

The Caring Leadership Framework

3

. . .

Look for the Greatness
in Those We Lead

Human ingenuity is unlimited, and leaders can unleash it.
Udaiyan Jatar, founder and CEO, Blue Earth Network

The caring leader prioritizes recognizing and then growing the gifts and talents of those he or she leads. Instead of ignoring the signs of greatness in their people, these leaders search for it. Then, just as an artist might do with his or her color palette, they go out of their way to amplify the unique gifts of those they lead. They meet with their people to ask what they can do for them instead of expecting performance without the proper care.

In *The 8th Habit: From Effectiveness to Greatness*, Stephen R. Covey explains that leaders must find their own "voice" and then help others find theirs. For Covey, voice represents a person's "unique personal significance," which is found by looking at their talent (what they are good at), passion (what excites them), conscience (the right thing to do or what they should be doing), and need (providing what they and the world needs for them to add value).[1]

In the context of the caring leader, looking for the greatness in those we lead allows us to help them find their unique personal significance. The caring leader does this for his or her people by allowing them to shine, giving them tools to grow, and believing in them and their potential.

Allow Them to Shine

Recently, my daughter took a rhetoric course, which required her to do speech analysis and deliver poems in front of her entire class. They all had to choose a speech, and she chose one by Malcolm X. This is my daughter—a quiet and compliant young lady—and she chose Malcolm X, an often controversial human rights activist. I asked her why.

She selected a Malcolm X speech on the Black revolution because the piece talked about getting the point across with people who are not listening. She believed in his lens. My daughter, who has had many learning delays to overcome in her life, was crystal clear about her decision.

She also said, "There were a lot of things that were against him. A teacher told him that he would never make anything of himself. I felt for him, because over my life, I had people who implied that I would not go places and that I couldn't do certain things. That really spoke to me."

After she gave the speech, her teacher and everybody else in the room was stunned! It was impactful for everyone, because it talked about the truth regarding a large group of people in America. For three or four days, her teacher continued to mention her talk in class in a positive light. Her teacher was so inspired that he even decided to do a unit on Malcolm X during the next semester.

I was surprised that my daughter took the step. I was so proud of her. Honestly, I'm not sure I would have had that courage. She decided to be her fullest self. She decided to be courageous in exploring what needs to be explored, teaching others, and helping them see another's truth. Her teacher put her in the position to shine and live to her strengths. Then, she rose to the occasion.

I love how Brigitte Grimm, chief deputy treasurer of Larimer County, provides a platform for her people to shine when she creates an environment in which they can innovate and take risks. Brigitte astutely described what those we lead really want: "People want to know that they are allowed to step out onstage, that they are allowed to try new things for the benefit of the customer and the team." Do not place limitations on your people. We need to put them in environments that allow them to stretch beyond themselves.

Timbra Yoakum, director of special programs for the Mabank Independent School District in Mabank, Texas, put it this way when defining her obligation to her people: "I help each person to find the leader within them, whether he or she may be a teacher or a direct assessments staff member. If they come to me with a problem, I want to hear their solutions first before I give them an answer." We have to provide environments for our people that allow them to stretch outside themselves, their limitations, and where they thought they could go.

When they stretch like this, whether they do well or not, we still recognize them for their courage, authenticity, and effort, because those are the things we value. When we value those things, then we get more out of our employees. As a result, they flourish.

Some years ago, I worked with a team member who was very nervous presenting to executive leaders. She was intimidated by their position. Unfortunately, in her role, she often presented to executive leaders. In my effort to help her get more comfortable with these presentations, I helped her think differently about these leaders. I helped her see that executive leaders were human just like her. Once she changed her mind about who they really were, and we worked together on her technique, she conquered her first presentation and won them over. I cared enough not to give her an excuse to fail. I wanted her to shine and succeed.

Some other ways to allow your people to shine might be delegating a project that you know highlights their strengths or asking them to do a presentation in your stead so that senior leaders can see your team members' brilliance. There are many ways to do this.

Whatever way you choose, be courageous like Brigitte and Timbra in exploring what needs to be explored, in teaching others, and in bringing them to the truth. Recognize your people for their courage, authenticity, and effort. Put them in positions to shine.

Another way to find the greatness in others is to give them the proper tools to grow outside of their comfort zone. When you intentionally provide your people what they need to advance, learn, and stretch, you help them grow in confidence.

Give Them Tools to Grow

Training

Sometimes, team members have so much in them but don't have the right tools to help them grow in or out of their current roles. The caring leader takes charge and makes sure to get those they lead the right tools for the journey. What do I mean by "tools"? Tools might mean that they have not had the right training, they might not have had the right access to decision-makers, or they might not have had the right feedback.

Rich Gassen, of the University of Wisconsin–Madison, was right on point when he shared, "So I've sought out training for some of the staff just so that they are better prepared and . . . they're on a path . . . to become a supervisor at some point in their career. So, making sure that they have the tools and resources available to interact with each other right now and in their future is important to me." What I love most about Rich's focus on arming his people with what they need to succeed is that he is the same person I highlighted in chapter 1 who proactively sought out the same resources for himself.

Rich chooses to show concern and kindness toward his team members on a consistent basis through everyday actions that help them grow. One other critical caring leader behavior is providing constructive feedback to those who look to us for guidance.

Feedback

One of the things that is missing most at work is consistent constructive feedback that allows employees to grow. Christina Wegner, vice president of marketing for the Vollrath Company, believes that feedback is a gift, and that leaders should curate an environment that provides a steady stream of formal and informal feedback to help people flourish.

Christina's practice is to sit and talk with her direct reports on a quarterly basis to review their performance plans. Additionally, midyear and at the end of the year, she sends out an informal 360 review to clients and coworkers of each of her direct reports to ensure that they stay on the right path forward. Of this cadence, Christina said that her team almost begs her for the feedback when they know it is coming. "They want to start working on the things that need improvement. And they want to make sure that they're continuing to evolve professionally and personally with their relationships internally." Christina's people appreciate the feedback, and it helps them discover their own greatness and opportunities for further growth.

I recall talking to one of my team members who seemed to be going through the daily routine with little gusto. I sat with her and let her know that I noticed her enthusiasm had waned. Also, I let her know that I saw she could be doing more in her career, and I found training that could help her advance. She was grateful and almost immediately demonstrated more energy for the work on which she was focused.

Ron Alvesteffer, CEO of Service Express, pointed out that leaders often miss the point that correcting team members is a sign of caring. Regarding this missed opportunity, Ron said, "I think the more you care, the more you can challenge them when appropriate. It's a balance of encouragement, coaching, and challenging." Ron reminisced about a teacher who "ripped him a good one" often. Ron said that he was his favorite teacher because he corrected Ron, and that showed Ron that he cared.

Rhoda Banks, vice president, head of talent management at Rabo AgriFinance, explained the importance of feedback in this way: "If you care about a person, and you want them to be successful, you will give them the honest feedback just like us as parents. We want to minimize or avoid hurt for our kids. So, we are constantly giving them advice. . . . The same is true in our leadership role. Although we are not their mom, we are caretakers of their future."

Honestly, while I do think of feedback as a gift, I never really thought of it as a tool. I love the openness on the part of Rich and Christina to learn and grow themselves—and, by extension, those they lead—by making sure they have what they need to move forward. Both Ron and Rhoda have the right idea. Feedback is just another way to show that we care. It's the best way to show concern and kindness for those we lead. Hand-in-hand with allowing them to shine and giving them tools to grow, caring leaders believe in those we lead, and we do all we can to help them live to their potential.

Believe in Them and Help Them Live to Their Potential

I have this gift that can sometimes get me into trouble. I notice the tiniest light inside of people even when others don't see it. Occasionally, I see more potential than is actually there: sometimes I believe that others are capable of much more than they can actually achieve. Nonetheless, I love trying to reveal that brilliance to others and grow that light so it shines brighter. I innately believe in people and their potential to want more and be more. When we believe in our team's potential and help them reveal it, we show them that we care for them, not just what they can do for us.

Many times, those we lead are not clear on what Judith Scimone, senior vice president and chief talent officer at MetLife, calls their "true authentic mission" and how and where to live it out to its fullest. Judith sees her role as catalyst to uncover her people's mission. She did not refer to organizational mission but to a "calling." According to Judith, the key for the leader is to help those they lead "fulfill that calling" no matter where they are sitting. For Judith, that team member may be able to fulfill it in the current organization or team, or in another organization. Either way, it is the leader's job to help those who look to them for guidance to find and follow that calling.

Rob Pepper, senior vice president of marketing at Excel Medical, shared a story with me about one of his team members that highlights the impact of believing in someone, maybe more than he believes in himself, and helping him live to his mission. Rob recalled a team member who was a graphic designer who he thought had the ability to be strategic enough to own the firm's entire digital presence. He remembered that his team member freaked out and seriously doubted she had what it took to take on such a huge role. Nonetheless, Rob assured his team member that he believed in her and that he would provide her with everything she needed to be successful.

Additionally, Rob shared that the team member followed him to two other workplaces when he moved on and is now very successful, working in a publicly traded company running the full digital strategy. As Rob explained, "They just needed someone to support them and believe in them. They had to believe in themselves. They had to be empowered to really get uncomfortable . . . to do more than their job. People just need to have a champion on their side."

Daniel McCollum, founder and CEO of Torrent Consulting, calls this unleashing of greatness "speaking the future into your people." Daniel explained that many people are afraid of the future. So, when the leader steps in and helps project a successful future for that team member, this "helps give them the courage to make decisions to take those little steps in the journey to develop them as a leader. We all need people in our lives . . . instilling some of that potential."

I had someone like that in my life who could see me going to law school before I could. She would encourage me and tell me how well I would do, which helped me visualize attending law school and being an attorney. I am not sure where I'd be today if she had not chosen to "speak the future" into me.

Leaders who have this as their focus, like Rob and Daniel, inspire those they lead to want more and be more. Through their daily actions to show concern and kindness to those in their organizations by genuinely believing in them, they demonstrate caring leadership.

Often, leaders don't always get it right. Being a caring leader does not insulate us from making the wrong decision and losing good employees. Steve McIntosh, founder and CEO of CML Offshore Recruitment, revealed to me a time when he missed the mark with one of his team members' potential. He struggled to get more out of this team member. The team member did not stay late or seem to be all-in with his work. He did not put energy into solving the organization's problems. Steve gave up on the team member, to his later regret. As a result, his team member left and became very successful at a new firm.

Steve vowed not to ever let that happen again. How does Steve ensure this? He sits down with everyone in the company every six months and talks about their advancement. He collaborates with them to uncover what has to happen for them to progress and make sure his company is meeting his team's expectations. He added, "It's a chance for us to share our expectations of them. And that we kind of make sure that no one is sitting out there just resenting their job and feeling like they're not moving forward in their career."

I am always inspired to hear from leaders who care about those they lead in the broader sense and not just for what the employees can do for them or their organization. In Steve's case, whether he realized it from the start or later, he knew that uncovering and then helping his people be all they could be was a key role of a caring leader.

Many of us need just one person to believe in our greatness and to help us unleash it. This has been true in my life. Believe in those you lead. Be the fuel to unleash a fruitful fire inside them that leads them to their best selves.

The Art of Caring Leadership in Practice

People choose to follow you because they know that you are looking out for them and that they can be, and live out, their best selves around you. Take the time to set up opportunities for them to shine, make sure that they have what they need to move forward, and, most important, believe in them enough to help them seek out what they are meant to do.

Caring Leader Highlight

Daniel McCollum
founder and chief executive officer, Torrent Consulting

Interviewed on: Episode 49, "Leaders with Heart Speak the Future into the People They Lead"

- **Industry/specialization:** Information technology and services

- **Aha moment:** After founding Torrent Consulting in 2010, Daniel saw tremendous growth in the first few years. As an entrepreneur, he was thrilled that his business was thriving, but he could tell that the company's rise would come at a cost. Sure enough, in 2017, Torrent Consulting went through a culture crisis. Daniel says his employees were beginning to lose trust in the company, and he knew his own leadership style wasn't resonating across the board. The next year, he committed to reassessing why he wanted to be a leader and dedicated more of his time to slowing down and connecting with his employees. Through this journey, Daniel realized that his core purpose is to love and serve people every day. He says, "I am really passionate about raising up leaders and giving that opportunity to all people regardless of economic status, race, religion, or where you're at in the world, so together we can make an impact on the world." He learned that bringing out the greatness in those he leads is a necessary step in bringing out the greatness of the company; in other words, people's success comes first, and the organization's success will follow.

- **How they embody caring leadership:** Chapter 3 wrestles with the challenge of looking for greatness in your employees and seeing potential in your organization where others may not. Daniel lives and breathes by this approach with his renewed leadership style, saying, "This thread of wanting to raise up other leaders is my personal outlet for loving and serving, where I feel I can bring the most value to the world." Once he transformed his company's outlook to a people-first strategy, he understood that uncovering the excellence in others gives his life greater purpose.

- **Guiding philosophy:**

  - People first is a strategy, not a nice-to-have. It's easy to see employees as simply the individual cogs in the vast machine that is the overarching company, but employees *are* the company and should be treated with the highest priority if you want your team to have any chance of succeeding. As CEO, Daniel counts this as his top responsibility: "I need to help give [employees] the opportunity to develop a voice to speak to both the company and the team."

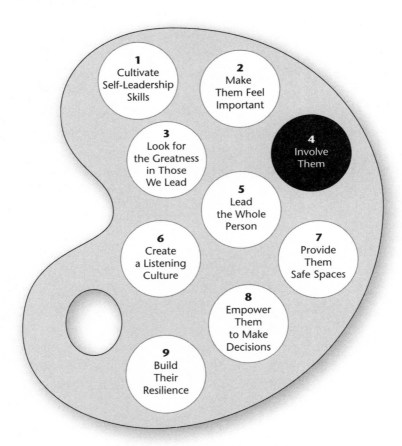

The Caring Leadership Framework

4

. . .

Involve Them

You have to interact, understand, encourage, and develop people, and
rely on them. You can get more through others than just through yourself.
Danielle Vaughan, president of compliance, FirstBank

Often leaders feel that the problems facing the business are theirs to solve
alone. However, when leaders tell their employees about the issues they
are facing, leaders see that they don't have to conquer the problems by
themselves. In fact, when they involve their employees in overcoming
whatever might be facing them and show vulnerability, it brings the team
closer together, and it helps the team see how they can contribute to the
solutions. It also gives the leader the grace to be imperfect when he shows
that he needs help.

When the leader is open and vulnerable about his need for help, he
learns to rely on his team, and they accomplish more together. Most important, he endears his employees to him even more, because the leader
shows that he is human.

The Canoe Lesson

Sometime ago, I was talking to my second-eldest son about the concept
of leading others. He is enrolled in Civil Air Patrol, which is the civilian
auxiliary arm of the US Air Force Academy. He is someone who could
do very well at the Academy, but he does not like to depend on others

to get things done. He does not like to work with and through others to accomplish his tasks.

While on vacation, my son went out in a canoe with his father. Afterward he said, "I was really nervous to be in there, because you really have to move at the same rhythm in order to get anywhere, or else you sit still or you go backward and the tide pulls you back in."

I said, "Well, you have to get on the same rhythm, because two people rowing in the same direction can get a lot farther than one rowing alone or two people rowing against each other. You'll go nowhere." He exclaimed, "But I would just rather be in a canoe by myself!"

What he said is really the crux of the struggle of a leader. Leaders must work with and through other people to accomplish things. In fact, the sign of a caring leader is one who can inspire those around her to achieve great things inside a team, and she involves them whenever possible. People do innovate by themselves, but great innovations come from cross-functional collaborations and teamwork. Leaders who foster that type of environment are much more effective in the workplace and, of course, at home.

I kept tapping the shoulder of my younger son to say, "Listen, yes, you have mental strength. You are intelligent. You are a great problem solver, but you have to empathize with others. You have to put yourself in the shoes of others, and you have to be OK with them not being perfect. You have to move forward when the waves are pulling against you. You have to work with the other person in the canoe." This was a great leadership lesson for my son.

Involving our team in the thinking and work that has to be done has a lot to do with allowing them to help shoulder the burden of that work.

Allow Them to Help Shoulder the Burden

I am a fast-moving person who drives for success. I also lead with my heart. Often, I am moving so fast that I outrun my own capabilities, and I have a hard time asking for help. When I take the time to pause, I release the need to control everything around me and invite others in. This is the only way I am successful in moving forward. Consequently, I learn often that I must allow others to help me shoulder the burden.

I adore the additional brushstrokes of color that Cheryl Fullerton, executive vice president of people and communications at Corus Entertainment, added when sharing her philosophy of including others. Cheryl believes that by involving those we lead in the problems to be solved, we will "get stronger people, who will dig into the problem and probably get better results. You'll build up their thinking ability, and you'll challenge your own assumptions about the principles that decisions are made on." It just makes sense to involve the entire team in the solutions we are seeking.

Scott McCarthy, an army logistics officer in the Canadian Forces and chief leadership officer at Moving Forward Leadership, a coaching consultancy, expanded upon the process that Cheryl described to include involving his people in an "after-action review." In his mind, when an incident occurs and things are done and settled down, he and his team conduct an after-action review, or debrief, where they ask themselves what happened, what went wrong, what they did right, and how they can improve.

Scott uses this method for minor mistakes, as a learning experience with his team. What does he do exactly? He mentions the mistake in a group meeting, and then the team, including the person who made the mistake, can go over it in an open manner to find out what they can do better next time. In Scott's words, "Now, you have someone who is operating . . . at a better level than they were two or three days ago." This style might seem harsh, but by involving his entire team in an open forum like this, he is creating a safe space in which to talk about the mistake.

As both Cheryl and Scott demonstrate, leaders strengthen those they lead when they involve them, not only by promoting a team focus but also by building up their ability to think critically and under pressure. This is also a confidence-builder that leaves people feeling a part of something bigger than themselves and cared for in the process.

If we want to effectively involve those we lead in making decisions and doing what is required, we must lean into their unique perspective.

Lean into Their Perspective

Mark Nagel, senior manager at Southwest Airlines, so brilliantly said, "Eighty percent of the results that we are looking for are within twenty feet of basically every problem that we are facing." This is such a crucial point to ponder.

Why do leaders either keep things in their inner circle or look outside for the answers they need? Often, we need go no further than our team members on the front line of the business. Daily, they are the ones who listen to customer compliments and complaints. They see which systems and processes work and which slow success. We must lean into their perspective.

Andrew McDonald, principal at Our Lady of Loreto Catholic School, completely understands this concept and discussed his "us" philosophy: "This is not about me; this is about us! So, if I am going to say that, then I need to live that." When Andrew has a big decision to make, he does what I talked about in chapter 2 and openly discusses the challenges that he and the school are facing with his team. He asks them what they think and gets their input into ways to overcome the challenges. He treats them as important members of the team.

Denise Testori, of Prestige Cleaners, leans in too by using her team as a sounding board for her own thinking. Denise first takes the time to write down her thoughts about what might not be meshing with the team and takes time to think about their perspective. Then she presents her ideas to the team and gets their feedback. Denise sees value in her team's perspective because she understands that it will be different from hers.

Being smart enough to know that you do not know everything as a leader of people is critical if you are to experience any level of career success. That's what's often referred to as the trait of humility, and it serves caring leaders extremely well.

I loved how Kevin Patterson, CEO of Connect for Health Colorado, framed this out, because he believes in the value of his people's perspective no matter where they sit in the organization. Kevin said, "No matter if it's the person at the front desk, the person on the phone, the person coming to pick up the trash, somebody's going to be able to give you a perspective that you did not have. . . . You've got to be open and listen to that, because you never know what one little piece is missing . . . that you needed to actually become clear on what the picture is."

One of the ways that I lean into the perspective of those I lead is to hold team roundtables to discuss a specific business issue. I go into the meeting with an open mind and heart, understanding that they most likely know more about the issue we are facing, given their proximity to the business. When I go to them with transparency and vulnerability, but with confidence in the solution, they really seem to appreciate it. This cadence brings us closer together.

When we lean into the perspectives of those we lead, we show them that we care about their opinion. We also show them that we value them as people. Another way we show that we care for them is by helping them make specific contributions to the team's success.

Help Them Make Contributions

DeeDee Williams, director of human resources at Davis, Graham & Stubbs, LLP, a law firm, said it beautifully: "At the end of the day, I cannot just assume that I am a great leader because of me. The people I work with contribute to the success of my leadership. They play a huge part in it." There are clear ways in which we can help our people make contributions to team success, from delegating to them in areas of their strengths to collaborating with them on projects that interest them.

Patty Salazar, executive director of the Colorado Department of Regulatory Agencies, shared a time when she had to rely on her team to make a significant contribution by standing in her place at a high-profile meeting that conflicted with another meeting she had to attend. Even though she used to try to do it all alone, she enlisted her team in a solution. Patty did what Andrew McDonald described above and was open with her core team about the challenges she was facing to garner different perspectives. As Patty said, "People are willing to step up and help you out when you're going through those challenges. . . . It really was just trusting my team and talking them through it and just learning how to ask for that support . . . just don't be afraid to ask for support from your village."

Patty gave her team an opportunity to show up for her and make a contribution that reduced the pressure on her to be in two places at the same time. This helped them to have more confidence. She did more than delegate—she involved them in the work that needed to get done. By being vulnerable and calling on her team to be a part of the solution, she demonstrated caring leadership.

Claude Silver, chief heart officer of VaynerMedia, seeks out ways to work directly with employees by asking someone to get involved in a project with her. She explained, "Either I will select them or I'll ask, 'Who wants to help me with the strategy right now?'"

DeeDee, Patty, and Claude understood that they could not do their jobs well if they did not allow others to make a specific contribution to team and organizational success. When leaders attempt to go it alone, there can be drastic consequences. Let's look at some examples of this.

Consequences of Not Involving Them

During each of my interviews, I invite the leaders to be vulnerable. This is a global podcast, and many of these leaders are sharing deep, rich stories for the first time. How do I do this? I assure them that I am not looking for perfect responses and that it will be a conversation as though we are sitting at a coffee shop. Moreover, I make sure to open up with rapport-building questions that allow my guests and me to get to know one another. I also share some of my own imperfect actions and experiences. This gives them permission to be open and transparent too. I am modeling the behavior I am seeking.

One example of this is when Alex Smith, chief human resources officer and chief change officer for the City of Memphis, shared the experience she had when she first started in her role and was going through her first budget process in front of the City Council. Admittedly, she was insecure. So, she decided to go about the budgeting process alone. She stayed late, did the research, and never involved the team. When she went to present the budget, she made mistakes. Fortunately, some of her team members were able to fill in the blanks. Nonetheless, she lost $100,000 out of her budget for that year.

This was a big lesson for Alex. Afterward, she started to embrace the idea of involving her team, not only so that she could tap into their knowledge base, but also so that they would "feel invested in the outcome." Alex handled the next budget year in a completely different way. She employed a very thorough process with the team to develop the budget and to study for the budget presentation so that they would be a part of the budget presentation process. As a result, Alex and her team were much more successful.

John LaFemina, executive director of performance management and chief risk officer at Pacific Northwest National Laboratory, had a similar experience of not enlisting his team's help and voice during a substantial project at the laboratory. As John described it, he was advocating for the laboratory leadership to spend $25 million on a new building. They were in an economic downturn, and things were looking tentative. His team advised him against moving forward at that time, but John ignored their advice. He was "focused on expanding the empire and building the business."

Unfortunately, when the Laboratory opened that building, they had no business, and it took two years to see a recovery. John had to be vulnerable and "admit where I screwed up." Luckily, his team forgave him. He knew that he needed them to help him move past this problem. Thankfully, with the help of his team, they were able to make a recovery. Of that time, he added, "I think I was able to survive that because, over time, I had made deposits in those relationships, built the trust, built that foundation for success." It was not John's imperfections that made him a caring leader. To the contrary, it was his subsequent admission of his mistake and inclusion of his team in the solution following his mistake.

These examples all provide a window into the importance of involving those we lead in the work that we do. Leadership can be tough work. Eyes are always on us. For everyone's benefit, let's be as inclusive as we can in the journey.

The Art of Caring Leadership in Practice

Everyone wants to know that they are a contributor to meaningful work. We want to know that we have an impact on our environment. As a leader, find ways to include those you lead in meaningful ways that help fulfill this need. When you do, you will immediately feel a shift in their desire to go over and above to achieve team and organizational success. Which projects are you giving away? With whom are you collaborating on work that must get completed? In what ways are you allowing others to make a contribution?

Caring Leader Highlight

Jennifer Butler
executive vice president and general manager, Innate Pharma

Interviewed on: Episode 6, "Why Leaders with Heart Know That They Cannot Do It Alone"

- **Industry/specialization:** Medical science (biotechnology)

- **Aha moment:** At one point in Jennifer's career, she was asked to manage a sales team of seventy people. She didn't have the experience of managing a sales team, so needless to say she was terrified. But Jennifer made the conscious decision to hide this fear and exude an exorbitant amount of confidence rather than reach out and ask for support. Only six months into her role, Jennifer received feedback that her team members could tell she was anxious and was desperately trying to hide it. However, this didn't make them respect her any less; in fact, it was the opposite. Her humanity inspired them. They told her that they trusted her vision and she only needed to let them into her process so they could best aid her and compensate for her lack of experience wherever needed. Jennifer reflected, "If I had just led from the heart, showing that I cared for them as individuals and as a team, providing support to enable and empower them, recognizing that they already have a great thing going on and I'm just there to bring a new perspective, that would have been so much better." After this wake-up call, Jennifer involved her team in more projects and decision-making processes and discovered a whole new support network that brought her leadership style to new heights.

- **How they embody caring leadership:** This chapter explains why leaders accomplish more when they are vulnerable about their need for help and open to relying on their team. Jennifer's story further highlights the need to be honest with our employees and how that transparency can enable leaders to connect on a deeper level with their peers. She argues that assuming a false sense of confidence just to do all the work yourself is essentially fear-based leadership, which ultimately serves no purpose: "Leading from fear and insecurity is not leading. . . . We lead from a secure sense of self." If you ask for help when you need it, that sense of self will be more stable than ever.

- **Guiding philosophy:**

  - *See feedback as the gracious gift it is.* Without the feedback Jennifer received, she might have continued to hide her insecurities and never ask for help. But because she respectfully received the constructive criticism that was extended to her, she felt the grace to be imperfect and ended up growing closer to her team as a result. She still leads with this tenet in mind.

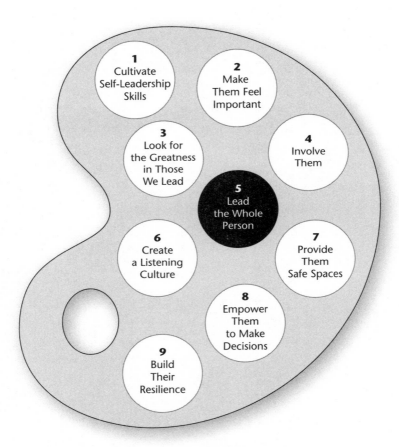

1
Cultivate
Self-Leadership
Skills

2
Make
Them Feel
Important

3
Look for
the Greatness
in Those
We Lead

4
Involve
Them

5
Lead
the Whole
Person

6
Create
a Listening
Culture

7
Provide
Them
Safe Spaces

8
Empower
Them
to Make
Decisions

9
Build
Their
Resilience

The Caring Leadership Framework

5

Lead the Whole Person

• • •

We need whole, real people in our workplaces. It's not only our
brain and body that should be present at work, but also our identities,
intuition, spirit, emotions, and our connections to each other.
Renée Smith, founder and CEO, A Human Workplace

Many leaders handle employees through a narrow lens of their performance inside the workplace without ever considering them as whole people and their lives outside of work. The caring leader understands that to get the most out of his relationships with those he leads, he must consider his employees' lives in total, including what is happening in their lives outside of work. This might mean helping them deal with mental health issues, brainstorming with them on which way to go with a child, or dealing with other personal issues. Leaders who lead with heart do not separate the person from what might be happening to him or her. On the contrary, they meet their employees where they are to help them achieve and be more.

Leading the whole person, then, means that we must take into consideration the mind, body, spirit, and emotions of those we lead. What in their personal and work lives adds to or takes away from their dimensions? They present one way at home. Do they feel safe to show up that way at work? Do we truly know them, or do we know their façades?

Sometime ago, I was blessed to chaperone a group of middle school girls at a faith retreat in the beautiful mountains of Colorado. What I enjoyed most about my time at this retreat were the small group sessions. My group was extra-special, since I had sixth- and seventh-grade girls;

many were in my son's class. I had watched them grow up. As a result, they were more comfortable with me. This environment was ripe for a leadership lesson on how to lead the whole person.

The weight of leadership was on my shoulders as I asked the girls questions and could see their reliance on me for the answers. I asked them questions of faith, personal identity, prioritization, and much more. Their answers were both innocent and transparent. I wanted to respond to them in that moment. Then, I needed to both show them compassion and remain strong when my heart hurt for some who expressed confusion and dislike for who they were and how they could best impact the world. More important, I knew I needed to meet them where they were, by disassociating my own feelings and experiences while also fully comprehending their own unique view. I held back tears after hearing their responses. Sadly, many felt unworthy, unfulfilled, that they didn't belong and were lost.

On my podcast and in my writing, I talk about the need to show our human side when our people are being vulnerable with us. Truthfully, I was the one being led. They exhibited caring leadership as they listened intently to the others present and responded with empathy.

The true meaning of "lead the whole person" came to a head for me that weekend. I left there feeling that I had created a safe space where they could air their fears, questions, and concerns without judgment. These young ladies wanted to find a place where they could be themselves and accepted for all their quirkiness. Certainly, I hope they found that in those small group meetings.

I will forever be grateful for that time. I will think of the girls fondly and pray that the best comes to them. My hope is that they will do what they were put on this earth to do, and that they answer that call with excitement and authenticity.

Leading others is a huge responsibility that cannot be taken lightly. Our people often look to us for guidance and a way around their challenges.

Why Lead the Whole Person?

When we meet our people where they are, we build trust with them. When they know that we understand them and the shoes they are standing in, they are more likely to meet us where we are, which requires a level of trust. Those we lead have a deep desire to feel safe and bring their full selves to work. When we accept them for what they bring to the table, including the baggage that we all carry; we empathize with them; and we pay close attention to the things that are important to them, they know it. They will grow from such relationship, model it to others, and be willing to do what it takes for the leader and the team to be successful.

Tom Dietzler of St. Peter Lutheran Church and School suggested "relationship building by walking around" instead of management by walking around to more fully understand those we lead. Tom's perspective is that we get to know those we lead by walking around and checking in on them so that we can meet their needs in that moment. Tom added, "While you're doing that, you're building trust with them. . . . If something does come up, they trust that you're going to handle it in a way that's even keel and not go off the deep end. . . . So, they get to know you, you get to know them, and that high trust is built."

This idea of building trust with our people to fully lead the whole person is a critical one. Our people will not feel comfortable sharing more of themselves with us until we have built that trust with them. Otherwise, fear of repercussions sets in, and a desire to hold back who they are takes hold. If they begin to act in this way, we lose our ability to tap into their full potential and help them achieve all they can be.

When we lead the whole person, we receive a gift to show up as our best self and help them do the same. As Ethan Mann, CEO of Validus Cellular Therapeutics, simply stated, "When your people come to you, when they ask for some flexibility and you're not able to give it to them, that's really the last chance you're probably going to get to actually support them."

Leaders must seize every opportunity to build trust and show support. One way that we do this is to accept our people as they come to us.

We need to be all right meeting them in their fullness. A significant part of doing this comes in our fully accepting who they really are.

Accept Those You Lead

When we are born into our parents' arms, we want them to accept us—flaws and all. We have a deep need to be seen and loved for who we are. To be *accepted* is to be "regarded favorably: given approval," according to Merriam-Webster.[1] Therefore, in a very real sense, if we do not feel accepted as a person, we feel rejected for all we represent.

When I was twenty-three years old, shortly after returning from a summer study abroad and pilgrimage to Israel, I had a jaw-dropping phone conversation with my grandmother that continued to drive home the fact that I was not a fully accepted member of my family. I was telling her about what a good time I'd had and the good people I'd met when staying in Jerusalem, in the Arab sector, and on a kibbutz. I mentioned something that for the life of me I cannot remember, and *bam!* I don't know what I said to strike a nerve, but she went off on me with the most hurtful words I had ever heard, which ended in, "You'd be a better Heather if your parents never married!" Whoa! We went back and forth for a while, and then I ended the call. After years of fighting for acceptance for who I was, this exchange made me realize that complete acceptance was not an option (read more about my story in chapter 9 under "My Story of Resilience").

From my many interviews, my conversation with Phil Cohen, founder and president of Cohen Architectural Woodworking, hit home and showed me what caring leadership really looks like. Phil showed such openness to accept employees who many would not think to hire (see the "Caring Leader Highlight" at the end of this chapter). Here is how he described the leader's responsibility to lead the whole person: "I think as a leader of teams, as a student, adviser, manager, director, VP, or executive, we have to be cognizant that people present with . . . their own unique lenses based upon their background, and we take that in when we bring them in as an employee. They don't just leave that at the door."

Regarding the need to foster an accepting workplace culture, Phil explained his thinking: "I know that as the CEO, I can do more to destroy a marriage than any counselor or therapist or pastor can do to repair it just by simply sending people home stressed out. So, we do everything we can to make sure they go home feeling satisfied." One of the ways Phil supports his employees is by offering classes on money management, how to advance themselves, and how to have a healthy and happy family. His team members even pass the envelope to help employees who might be struggling financially. Phil understands what it means to lead the whole person. He sets aside casting any judgments on how his people show up. Instead, he opens his heart to the possibilities.

I adored how Sarah Bernhardt, vice president of people at Greystone Technology, a medium-size technology consulting firm, expressed her feelings around concerning ourselves with all aspects of those we lead as they present to us: "If I'm struggling at home, my kid is sick, my husband is struggling, and life is just harder at home, it becomes tougher to put on that game face at work. . . . I invest in the folks that I'm working with, and I really want them to be happy, successful, growing, and feeling good about stuff." Just as Phil does, Sarah embraces all of what her people represent. By consistently allowing the whole person to take shape, both Phil and Sarah demonstrate caring leadership.

We are whole people no matter where we go. Jill Katz, founder and chief change officer at Assemble HR, a small human resources consultancy, expressed it wonderfully: "It doesn't do anything productive for anyone involved for us to be keeping parts of who we are outside of our job." Expecting a separation of the parts of us before we enter through different doors sets up unhealthy parameters, a lack of confidence, and disconnection. No team or organization can thrive through that.

Often the issue is that leaders feel uncomfortable taking in personal information or feelings of those on their teams. Part of it stems from the leader's fear of having to share personal parts of herself. Many years ago, I remember going into a new management role. One day, when I was relaying a piece of information the team needed to know about my personal life, one of them exclaimed, "Wow! We didn't even know our prior manager got a divorce from his wife until a couple of years after it was final!" I was dumbfounded by their prior manager's lack of transparency and vulnerability. I took this type of vulnerability for granted. My team truly appreciated knowing more about me. As stated in chapter 2, "Make Them Feel Important," leaders must strike the right balance between selective sharing that helps the team move forward and oversharing, which could affect team morale and performance.

Accepting those we lead for who they are is an important part of leading the whole person and removes any barriers to their being their authentic selves. Another very important brushstroke to add is that we must learn to stand in their shoes and empathize with what they are facing.

Show Empathy and Compassion

Some years ago, I took a position running customer experience for a local government. I was excited about this new opportunity to impact the entire customer journey. Soon after taking the position, I realized the limitations that were inherent in my role. I was frustrated, to say the least. One day, my manager, sensing my frustration, came down to my office, unannounced, and with a big smile on his face sat down in the chair across from me and said, "I know that you are frustrated, because you feel like the leadership team is stopping you from doing what you do best. I just want you to know that we hired you to do exactly what you are doing, and we appreciate you. Just keep your chin up, OK? And have patience with us. Keep up the good work!" I wanted to hug him right then, because he had met me where I was with compassion and empathy. He noticed where I was in my shoes, and he made me feel cared for and valued. That was caring leadership at its finest.

Empathy and compassion are critical leadership skills. The manager I just described was masterful in exhibiting both. Merriam-Webster defines *empathy* as "the action of understanding, being aware of, being sensitive to, and vicariously experiencing the feelings, thoughts, and experience of another of either the past or present without having the feelings, thoughts, and experience fully communicated in an objectively explicit manner."[2] *Compassion* is "sympathetic consciousness of others' distress together with a desire to alleviate it."[3]

While these two expressions of care are underrated, they can be overused. Empathy and compassion are my biggest strengths, predominately because of my childhood, which heightened my ability to see who was authentic, or truly cared for me, and who was mostly self-serving. In my management career, both qualities have mostly served me well. Nonetheless, there have been times when I got too close to someone else's pain and became overly zealous in trying to alleviate it.

Up until I was about thirty-five years old, I found myself exhausted from my level of effort to advocate for anyone who needed me. I wanted to come to their aid. What I discovered was that I needed to be selective in my empathy and compassion or else I would burn out. So, I chose to empathize and, in some cases, act on the empathy, but I got better at disassociating my friends' challenging circumstances from an obligation to solve them. I also did much of what I talked about in chapter 1 under "Exercise Self-Care," and I focused on caring for myself and replenishing myself. All elements of the palette work together to demonstrate caring leadership.

As empathy and compassion are so important to leading the whole person, I really appreciated how Greg Wathen, president and CEO of the Economic Development Coalition of Southwest Indiana, models both of these skills when figuring out how to help meet the needs of his people: "I take some time to sit down and think from that other person's perspective. . . . That helps me understand what challenges that we need to try to address to understand what they're going through, and then how do we address them moving forward. But until you ask the question, until you have the conversation, you really just never know."

Benilda Samuels, vice president of programs at Rose Community Foundation, takes this thoughtful others-focused process and adds in her own personal experience as a place to start meeting her people where they are: "When people call me and say, 'Can I work from home, because I have this issue with the baby and I got kicked out of day care' . . . to me,

I completely get it and there's no reason to add to that stress, because I know that I've been there, and I know that things have changed for me. I tell them that all the time."

Adding to the focused effort to empathize by Greg and the gift of experience from Benilda, Rich Gassen of the University of Madison–Wisconsin demonstrated great empathy when he decided to help out one of his team members who was also a high school football coach when Rich noticed that his team member's communication to the parents of the football players was lacking. As you saw in chapter 1, Rich takes control of his own education and growth. He does the same for those he leads.

Rich sent his team member to a couple of classes that benefited him as a football coach so that "he was better aligned with handling those situations, because he was struggling early on as a football coach." Rich saw that helping his team member outside of work also allowed his work team to benefit.

Greg, Benilda, and Rich all showed the perfect blend of empathy and compassion for those who looked to them for concern and kindness. These leaders demonstrated how to not only sense another's pain or circumstances but also add action to the mix to alleviate it. Another essential way to lead the whole person is to pay attention to the details of his or her life. When we miss the details, we often miss the opportunity to lead our team members the way they prefer.

Pay Attention to the Details

Leading the whole person is not a scalable concept. It is building individual relationships with our people and paying close attention to the details of their lives. What do they like? What do they dislike? What are their biggest dreams? What are their biggest fears? What are they grappling with right now? Andy Books, sales manager of Salelytics, showed that he gets this concept when he explained, "I'm about trying to engage them on a personal level and being able to understand what drives them and what motivates them. I mean, some people want to be able to excel at the highest points of the organization—I think that's important. We need to be able to give them the tools to get there."

Mareo McCracken, chief customer officer at Movemedical, said, "Leadership is conversations, and how well you lead is determined by how good those conversations are." According to Mareo, to meet the needs, wants, and desires of those we lead, we must have conversations that meet something in every one of them. How do we do this? We need to determine their communication style and preferences. We can do this by using formal assessments, such as DiSC®, or we can combine this with just getting to know more about them. Are they very verbal people who like to talk things through? Do they like to get straight to business minus niceties? As Mareo alluded, if we have the wrong kinds of conversations with our people, we could throw them off and cancel out any trust built.

Andy Books, mentioned above, shared a great example about a vice president in his organization who understood that a huge part of showing we care about others has to do with the details we remember about their lives and accessing those details at the right time. Andy and some of the senior leaders in his organization were bringing on a new client. Andy recalled that they were just starting a call with the new client, whose wife and children, unbeknownst to Andy, had been in a car accident just a few days before.

One of Andy's VPs exclaimed, "OK, before we get into this, let's talk about what's important. Joe, how's the family? How are the kids? How is everybody doing?" The client representative briefly talked about the accident and what had happened and at the end said, "Thank you for asking." The VP said, "You know, I'm really glad you're here, that everybody's OK. We need to focus on the important things in life!" This exchange impacted Andy. It is also a great example of accessing important details in a way that shows you care. This VP showed this new client that she cared and modeled it for others to emulate.

Ray Aguirre, chief of police at California State University, Fullerton, believes that showing true care and concern also pays off in better performance and increased trust. Here is what he does with this team to ensure that he knows what is going on in their lives and that they know he cares:

- He makes sure to start each meeting or exchange by asking about how they are doing and what is going on in their lives. If he knows that someone is ill in their family, he will ask how they are doing. He goes deeper than what is on the surface at work.

- He sends a birthday card to every member of his department when it's their birthday.

- Whenever a family member of one of his team members passes away, or they themselves are in the hospital, he reaches out to them and sends flowers.

T. Renata Robinson, PhD, chief human resources officer at Colorado Coalition for the Homeless, knows all too well what it's like to show up for those inside her organization. Here is what she shared: "Working for a homeless organization, the people in the organization have experienced homelessness and they have their own trauma, and then they are dealing with clients with trauma. That's a lot to deal with." Renata shared that her employees receive "a whole lot of love and a whole lot of care." She might offer a day off or the ability to work offsite if the employee is going through a tough time. That is a hard spot to be in, but as Renata said, "building relationships to support people" is her focus.

Mareo, Andy, Ray, and Renata all help dispel any doubts that leaders with heart exist. They meet their people where they are by accepting them, empathizing with them on their journey, and paying attention to the details of their lives.

The following is an example of what happens when we do not pay attention or exercise emotional intelligence when interacting with those we are supposed to lead.

Second Chances

Heather Heebner, vice president of human resources at Instant Financial, an earned wage access platform for employees, told me about a time when she was not very proud of her leadership. She was meeting weekly with her direct reports by phone, and one of them repeatedly expressed frustrations. Heather was not in a good place because the organization was strained for resources and HR had very little support. With each call with her direct report, she tried to redirect the conversation to a more positive outlook instead of going deeper and seeing the clues of the person's discontent. After one tough phone call, Heather's team member resigned from the company.

Heather regrets that conversation because, as she said, "I wasn't there for my team member. When I look back in hindsight, I should have recognized the clues sooner, and instead of trying to turn things into a positive note on each and every call, I should have really gone and said, 'What's going to be what makes you proud to work here?' . . . I think we as leaders miss the clues." Heather is not a perfect leader. None of us are perfect. Continue reading to see her leadership evolution.

Some years ago, (as shared in Chapter 1) I worked in an organization that was going through a merger. Things were getting rocky. Many of the leaders left their employees in the dark. As a result, employees made assumptions and mistrust ran rampant. Rightfully, people were afraid of losing their jobs. Unfortunately, the merger was not going well. The organizational leaders decided to initiate layoffs. As one of the more highly paid employees, I was in the first round of layoffs. There were a few more rounds after I left. The layoff process, though painful, left me feeling that I still mattered. My boss showed true empathy as he broke the news. The HR team was supportive and accessible.

Heather Heebner, the leader I introduced above, was the human resources lead for the entire merger. Heather knew that I had four children, but she did not know that my husband had quit his job two weeks before and his insurance covered our entire family. You know what she did? She found a way to add my family to the company's COBRA for the next three months to make sure we were covered. She picked up the bill!

Prior to the layoff, Heather and I were distant colleagues who had the same name. After that layoff and what she did for my family, we were friends. I wanted to share this counterexample with you so that you could see that Heather is a caring leader despite her oversight in the first example. Caring leadership requires that we get better every day. It does not require perfection. Heather could have ignored my needs in that moment. Instead, she met me where I was and left me feeling cared for. In a funny twist, she helped me find my calling and endorsed my first book on employee loyalty.

The Art of Caring Leadership in Practice

We all love to be seen and accepted for who are, and want others to understand where we are coming from. Take some time to sit with one of your team members today and just listen to her. Ask her how she is doing and what obstacles are in her way.

A Caring Leader Highlight

Phil Cohen

founder and president, Cohen Architectural Woodworking

Interviewed on: Episode 69, "Leaders with Heart Invest in the Potential of Their People"

- **Industry/specialization:** Architecture (woodworking)

- **Aha moment:** Phil's moment of reckoning was decades in the making. Before founding Cohen Architectural Woodworking, Phil was homeless and suffering from a substance abuse problem. He turned to woodworking for its therapeutic qualities, starting with small projects that gave him peace of mind. Soon his company picked up momentum with larger projects, and he hasn't looked back since. They are now at seventy employees with a 55,000-square-foot facility. However, Phil carries his storied past with him as a leader. He knows that in order to be an authentic leader, he needs to share those tough but meaningful life experiences and the many lessons he learned along the way. Phil explained that he looks at the whole person when hiring employees. "From the beginning, we've always hired people with a bad past. People who were like me—people who had a past felony, people who had a past with drugs, people who have been through trauma, people who are uneducated. . . . We tell them, 'We don't care where you came from. As long as you draw a hard line on that, you have strong work ethic, and you develop your character, we'll help you get there.'" By looking at each team member through a holistic lens and giving him or her a chance, Phil builds a diverse team with unique strengths and strong emotional skills. He doesn't discriminate based on people's backgrounds or lowest moments; rather, he welcomes those possible negatives to the table and leverages them as positives.

- **How they embody caring leadership:** As chapter 5 elucidated, the caring leader knows he must carefully consider the entirety of his employees to get the most out of their relationships, and that includes such things as their identities, their pasts, and their personal lives. Phil models this behavior on a regular basis, connecting with his employees on matters that extend well beyond the workplace. He welcomes this kind of open dialogue, explaining, "We have a half-day orientation for our people where I tell them my story and they tell theirs." By leading the whole person (and not just the employee side), Phil inspires his employees to do their best work, day in and day out.

- **Guiding philosophy:**

  - *Recognize employees for their potential, not their missteps.* Phil's inclusive hiring practice shows without a doubt just how committed he is to seeing the best in people. Giving others a chance when no one else will has ultimately added a new shade of purpose to his own life beyond woodworking: "My whole purpose of being here is to help change people's lives and change their families."

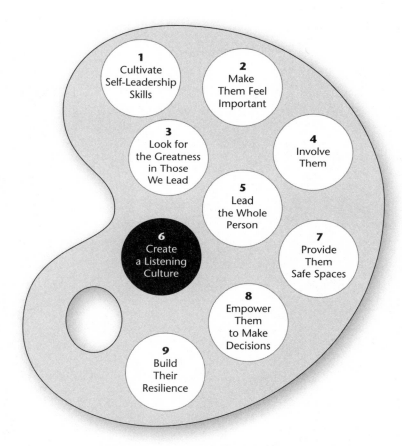

1
Cultivate
Self-Leadership
Skills

2
Make
Them Feel
Important

3
Look for
the Greatness
in Those
We Lead

4
Involve
Them

5
Lead
the Whole
Person

6
Create
a Listening
Culture

7
Provide
Them
Safe Spaces

8
Empower
Them
to Make
Decisions

9
Build
Their
Resilience

The Caring Leadership Framework

6

Create a Listening Culture

• • •

I make sure that people from every level feel like they are
being heard, that their ideas are not just being pushed aside.
D'anthony Tillery, AVP, talent acquisition, Atrium Health

Listening is a vital skill for everyone—in particular, the caring leader. Yet it is far easier to talk about listening than it often is to listen effectively. Why? Because poor listening skills abound in our organizations. Whether it's due to a lack of interest in the subject matter, distractions, impatience, laziness, or a host of other possibilities, we often talk about listening more than we seek out and polish best practices for creating a listening culture.

Why is listening so important? We all have an innate desire to be heard. Our voices are a significant part of what makes us us! When those whom we look to for guidance fail to listen and respond to our voices, it's as though they are rejecting a part of us. In an environment where we feel listening is lacking, we feel less fulfilled—that the work we do has less meaning and the people around us don't care for us fully.

Caring leaders create a listening culture that is bidirectional, responsive, and supportive. They use the voices of their people to improve the workplace for all. These leaders know that listening alone is not enough. Employees feel powerful when they know that their feedback will be acted upon, even just some of the time.

What is a listening culture? It is one that involves using what I refer to as "The Cycle of Listening" (see figure 1), wherein leaders are actively listening to those they lead, processing what they hear, potentially acting upon some of the feedback, and then communicating back to the original feedback source along the way. The Cycle of Listening never ends. It cannot if we are to know that our voices are powerful!

Organizationally, there are three main approaches to listening in organizations: First, the leader schedules and then attends consistent one-on-one meetings with each team member inside and outside of the performance review process. Second, the leader listens to his or her entire team in team meetings or roundtables. Third, leaders listen at the organizational level, using surveys, focus groups, culture teams, and interviews.

In listening, the first step is seeking to understand, and this requires active listening. In the organizational sense, the listening becomes active through the motion in the cycle. In the individual sense, active listening is as Claude Silver, of VaynerMedia, described it: "I would suggest asking open-ended questions so that you can glean what that person really has to say." When leaders practice active listening by first seeking to understand, and even repeat back what they hear, those they lead feel heard and valued.

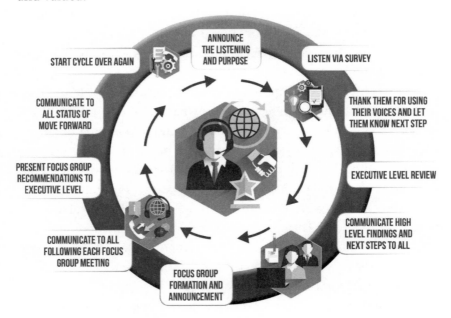

Figure 1. The Cycle of Listening

Seek to Understand

A huge part of active listening is seeking to understand another person, without an agenda and with a service mindset. As Arlene Mendoza, senior innovation program manager at Alluma, so astutely proclaimed, "Listening to understand is a whole different dynamic, because it's about extracting and understanding what the other person is trying to communicate to you." The opposite of seeking to understand is making a decision that affects others without seeking their input and making assumptions about others' wants and needs.

Chuck Runyon, cofounder and CEO of Self Esteem Brands, experienced firsthand what happens when we forget to gather input from others. The company that Chuck cofounded was growing a lot, and he and his cofounder were moving fast. Chuck presented the launch of a major initiative at a franchise conference. He had not done a good job of taking input from franchise owners ahead of this launch. As a result, the audience did not rally around this new initiative.

At that moment, Chuck learned that he had to be better at including all stakeholders up front and in advance of any major decisions. Of that experience, he shared, "It starts with seeking to understand everyone's perspective. You can't keep everyone happy—that's a recipe for disaster—but you'd better be able to explain, in detail, that you heard them, you understand them, and here's why the company is going in this direction."

Chuck has a renewed outlook on the importance of including those who look to him for guidance and support. As I make clear on my podcast, caring leaders are not perfect. They just happen to be more emotionally intelligent, in that they sense the concerns of others and they respond by showing concern and kindness in return. Chuck courageously showed us how this looks.

Sarah Bierenbaum, founder and principal of Sarah B Consulting, shared a time with me when her team provided feedback on their frustrations around interdepartmental communication and internal team communication within a high-growth environment. In that process, her team came up with ideas, Sarah and her colleague reflected on their next steps, and Sarah's colleague was set to present their ideas to the larger team. On the day of the presentation, her colleague could not attend. So, Sarah presented the idea in her place.

Unfortunately, Sarah botched the presentation, because instead of pointing to the fact that the plan came from the ideas of the team, she just stated that management had ideas and professed what they were going to do and what would work best. She immediately sensed a change in her team's energy in the negative direction. Following the meeting, she knew she had work to do. So, she set up one-on-one meetings with her direct reports. She admitted that she had made some mistakes by failing to let her team members know that the next steps were directly tied to their previous feedback. Then, she asked them what they thought she had done wrong.

By being open and asking for feedback, Sarah received it, and she used that feedback to listen and respond more effectively. Of that experience she said, "I feel like that was a monthlong class on being a better leader."

Personally, I move very fast in and out of projects and even in and out of thoughts. Sometimes, this makes those around me feel that they are not a part of the process. Often, I feel myself going into hyperdrive. Then I slow myself down and begin to see the others who are with me on this journey. I know that I need to include their voices and their input. I am not always great at executing on that. I continue to work on this, and because it is so important to me, I make it a priority. Nonetheless, like both Chuck and Sarah, I must recommit to seeking to understand those around me before taking any action. The caring leader does this and then reflects on what he or she hears.

Reflect on What You Hear

Taking time to reflect on any type of feedback we hear allows us to process it and decide what actions, if any, we will take. This reflection can be done alone or within a team environment. Responding too quickly can mean that we have not considered the information's validity or alternative paths. Taking too long to reflect and respond could cause apathy. In short, timely, well-thought-out feedback is critical for building and maintaining trust.

I work with organizations on creating a strong Cycle of Listening (see figure 1) so that employees' voices are heard and acted upon, when appropriate. Because I have read thousands of employee survey comments and sat in on almost one hundred focus groups, I see the energy rise in employees when they realize that what they have to say matters and that those who lead them take their feedback into consideration.

While listening is critical, leaders must discern what feedback they will act upon. As Jo-Ann Robertson, CEO of Ketchum London, explained, "That doesn't mean that I take every piece of feedback I get as gospel, but I always listen to them. Then, I reflect on whether I think it is fair or not, and whether I think I should do something about it or not." This is an important point, because often organizational leaders shy away from putting an employee feedback process in place.

Often, leaders feel that they need to respond to everything, and thus they respond to nothing. Given my experience, employees are adults. They understand that there are many moving parts to the business to which they are not privy. Therefore, they know that organizational leaders cannot make every possible change they request. Nonetheless, taking some action speaks volumes to them about the value you place on their voices.

Affirm through Action

When we think about the Cycle of Listening, we will fall short if we never act on what we hear. Many organizational leaders listen via the mediums I already described and then have no intention of acting. This inaction produces mistrust and apathy on the part of employees.

I am not arguing that we must react to or change everything we hear in feedback. To the contrary, I am suggesting that we be thoughtful before deciding not to act. I love how Kevin Patterson, CEO of Connect for Health Colorado, works through this process with those he leads after he receives their feedback. Kevin starts off by saying, "OK, let me make sure

I understand what you're saying." Then, he tries to respond in a way that he does not overpromise but also lets them know that he heard the message. He knows this method works because people often come back to him and say, "I can see you heard what I said, because this is different now."

You can see why Kevin is a caring leader. He respects what his people have to say. He does not discount any of their voices. Additionally, he is thoughtful in acting on what he hears.

If we seek to understand and are thoughtful about what we hear as Kevin is, we will leave those we lead feeling heard and important. When we take it one step further and consistently connect the dots for those who provide us feedback, we amplify the confidence and self-worth of our people.

Connect the Dots

When I refer to connecting the dots, I really mean that leaders need to communicate what they hear during moments of feedback and what they intend to do about what they heard. So, every time leaders take an action directly related to employee feedback, they need to let the employees know that their actions are directly connected to that feedback. If they do not do this, they lose an opportunity to show employees how much they care, how powerful their voices are, and that organizational success is a team effort. This might seem simple for some, but I am stunned by how little organizational leaders communicate back to those who provide any type of feedback. This lack of bidirectional communication is why many employees opt out of surveys and feedback sessions.

Phil Burgess, chief people and operations officer at CSpace, connects the dots in a thoughtful way that leaves those he leads feeling validated. Here is how Phil describes his process of listening:

> I do really try to listen to people, and then think about what is the action we need to drive as a result. And I'm learning that the more you communicate and connect the dots back to people, and help them understand that as a result of the conversation I had with them, I've been able to have a conversation with my

boss and trigger an initiative around well-being or make some progress on diversity and inclusion, then I think connecting those dots starts to help people feel that you're making progress. I think the more you do it, the more they then also forgive you when you get stuff wrong.

What touched me most about my exchange with Phil was that he is eager to get better, by including others, being thoughtful about the big picture, and showing the right balance of care for those he leads. Connecting the dots, or consistently and strategically communicating as described above, is one of the most important things leaders can do to ensure that a culture of listening stays intact. Creating this type of culture elevates the experience from the caring leader to the caring organization.

The Art of Caring Leadership in Practice

From the time we are babies, we love to hear our own voices, and we love to see those whom we look to for guidance, safety, and love respond to our words. You have the power to make those you lead feel heard. Commit to actively listening to them more often. Confirm your understanding by repeating back what you hear. You might be surprised by what you uncover.

Caring Leader Highlight

Chuck Runyon

cofounder and chief executive officer, Self Esteem Brands

- **Interviewed on:** Episode 77, "Leaders with Heart Understand That There Is an Emotional Investment to Being a Leader"

- **Industry/specialization:** Health, wellness, and fitness

- **Aha moment:** Chuck often says he's a completely different leader now as CEO of a global franchise than he was as the founder of a small start-up. That meteoric rise to corporate success taught him countless leadership lessons and brought him face-to-face with the never-ending challenges of effectively leading hundreds of employees. He recounted one experience that shifted his thinking: "I remember launching a major initiative at our annual conference in 2009, and I just didn't do a good job of taking in the input and feedback of our franchise owners prior to this launch," Chuck confessed. "And it was too aggressive, it was too fast." Chuck admitted that he could feel the audience's less-than-receptive energy, and soon top executives confronted him about where they disagreed. At its root, the main problem was that Chuck had failed to listen to his company. He eventually had to put the initiative on pause, reconnect with his various franchisees, and listen to feedback. Soon he was able to retool his project with the full support of the company, now that he had demonstrated that he was committed to heeding their concerns and ideas. Chuck said that he now leads with open ears: "A lot of times, [other teams] are creating the plan, and we're just helping them as sounding boards since we see the business in different areas." With the value of active listening firmly in the fore of his leadership approach, Chuck continues to see innovation from those around him.

- **How they embody caring leadership:** This chapter illuminates why a listening culture is paramount for any leader's success. Chuck's own story of failure to listen proves that employees simply aren't willing to support leaders of an environment where they feel that listening is lacking. He now recognizes that listening is the secret weapon to making employees feel fulfilled and committed to their work. Chuck said, "Founders come up with ideas. Leaders become cheerleaders for others' ideas." To cheer on the ideas of others, you must be open to hearing them first.

- **Guiding philosophy:**

  - *A leader's job is to take the time to listen to everyone and harvest the team's best ideas from there.* As Chuck reaps the benefits of a listening culture at work, he knows that his job has fundamentally shifted. "There are teams who are more capable and smart, and it's my job just to harvest all the great ideas going on. Afterwards I edit them and make sure that they have the right resources to carry it out." With all the strengths of your employees, it would be a wasted opportunity not to use them. Release the shame of not being the loudest voice in the room.

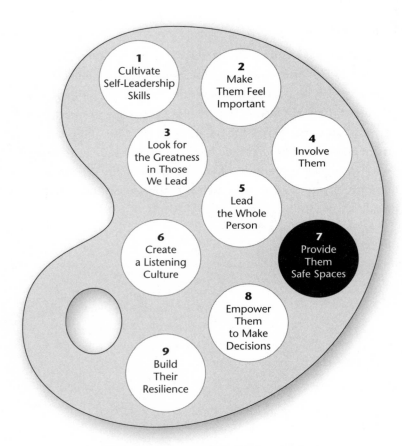

The Caring Leadership Framework

7

Provide Them Safe Spaces

• • •

There has got to be a shared trust that what you have created is a safe environment for your people, because if not, it can slow everything down.
Chris Chancey, founder and CEO, Amplio Recruiting

In my research, one common thread is that employees don't always feel safe to express their true thoughts, share ideas that might be counter to the mainstream, or discuss things that make them feel uncomfortable for fear of some type of attack or retribution. Those who lead with heart make sure to create spaces in which to have conversations where employees can feel psychologically safe and protected from microaggressions.

When I refer to safe spaces, I mean spaces free of fear and ridicule and where those we lead are free to express their opinions and concerns. After reading this chapter, you will begin to see how all chapters build on and depend upon one another. In chapter 5, I pointed out the importance of leading the whole person, and in chapter 6, I pointed out how creating a listening culture makes people feel important and heard. Neither of those is possible without first creating a safe space. Before we can expect to have or create safe spaces, we must earn trust.

Earn Trust First

To create a safe space where others can speak up and pose questions or present countering views, they must trust those in the room and in the organization. Leaders do not get trust because of their title; they earn trust by how they treat those they lead and how they make them feel. As Sheryl Simmons, CEO of 3flightsHR, perfectly stated during our interview,

> When they trust you and you've created that space for them, they're going to raise their hand when things are going sideways, because they trust you to handle it and they trust you to do what's best for both them and the company. . . . But you have to intentionally curate those relationships and take the time to create that emotional bank account and make a deposit so that they feel safe coming in and having those conversations.

A study by Quantum Workplace found that only 39 percent of employees were being emotionally transparent around senior leaders and executives.[1] Trust is earned, and the caring leader understands that she must take an active role in earning it. The other side of this equation is that once we build that trust, we understand that the feedback is a sign of the strength of our relationships.

Melissa Eovine, manager of sponsorships for the Fellowship of Catholic University Students, added some rich texture to this concept: "Build rapport and respect with your team so that they will feel safe to be vulnerable. To those that I lead, I believe we have enough respect for each other that we know if we bring something up, it's not attacking the person. It's actually saying we want what's best for each other, and it's built on that respect and safety."

What are some clear ways to create a safe space? As a manager of teams for the majority of my career, I did three things consistently to make sure that my people felt safe to open up about who they were and what they were thinking on a variety of topics:

1. When one of my team members provided feedback, either one-on-one or in a team meeting, I would actively listen to him and then make sure to include his thoughts, in some way, in a decision I needed to make. That way, he would hear his voice in our go-forward strategy. This gave him confidence to continue to speak up, and it also let him know that I valued him.

2. Often, I would poke fun at myself for thinking or acting in a certain way. I did this, first, because I wanted team members to know that I did not take myself too seriously. Second, I wanted them to see me as the human being that I was and not as some perfect person who never messed up. This vulnerability brought them closer to me.

3. I am both a relator and an empathetic person. These two strengths served me well on my leadership journey, since most of us want to deal with people who can relate to us and can empathize with our situation. I found that the more I grew these skills, the more people knew they could come to me when they would not go to others. I did not take this for granted but knew that I needed to use what I discovered to improve their experience in some way.

Another way to create safe spaces for those we lead is to create a culture where speaking the truth in a respectful way is expected and even applauded.

Make Speaking the Truth the Norm

I was quite impressed with P. Joseph O'Neill, CEO of G&D Integrated, as he spoke about his philosophy around speaking the truth. Joe believes that "truth has to be the currency of our realm." Here is what Joe said about this concept: "People respond extremely well when they realize that they can say what's on their mind. Whatever you say, say it respectfully. It doesn't mean every conversation is going to be easy, fun, or pleasant, but we're all going to speak our truth, and only by doing that can we express our respect for each other."

This notion of speaking the truth is a hard one, especially for leaders who often have a fluffed-up idea that their team members see them as perfect. Then, they start to believe it or are afraid of the team members' discovering otherwise. In this context, many leaders are threatened by the idea of creating a culture of speaking the truth. Joe tells us to embrace it, as it is also wrapped in respect.

A critical path to creating a safe space for open dialogue is to actively invite those who tend to be quiet or keep their thoughts to themselves to speak, whether in front of others or behind the scenes.

Invite Them to Speak

In my conversation with LaToya Lyn, vice president of Talent Strategy at Oscar Health, she recalled always feeling that she needed an invitation to go to meetings. She is an African American woman, and as she recalled, she was often left off of meeting invites. After a while, she just decided to invite herself. You know what happened? Nothing. She wasn't yelled at or thrown out. This made me think more deeply about this idea of inviting people to the table.

While I don't think many would take on the same show-up-anyway mindset, I do think that as leaders, we must first create an environment that is inclusive of all voices. It's easy for us to invite those we like or those who look like or act like us. Nonetheless, our invitations, whether implicit or explicit, must advance and include the whole.

During my conversation with Mark Nagel, senior manager at Southwest Airlines—HR transformation/employee services, he helped me to see that safe spaces come from feeling safe. For us to feel safe, we need to know that our voice is welcome and matters. In my childhood, I don't recall anyone asking me for my opinion about what was happening around and to me. Mark helped me realize that this had made me feel unsafe—or, as I call it, uncared for. That is why I am so focused on being the bridge to help others feel heard and safe.

Therapy talk aside, Mark presents a compelling scenario for us to consider when trying to help those we lead to feel safe. Mark's approach is simple: "When you look around the table, if you know someone who doesn't talk, ask them, 'What do you think?' Invite them to the table." Mark takes it a step further when someone in the circle says, "Well, it's just my opinion." He stops the person in that moment and says, "Don't say, just your opinion. By saying 'just,' you're minimizing your opinion. Your opinion matters just as much as, if not more than, anybody's at this table. So, don't minimize your opinion."

Wow! That is a powerful practice, isn't it? When he takes those pauses, he is not only creating a safe space but modeling what other leaders should do. He is also showing concern and kindness to someone who needs to know he or she is valued. The other practice that Mark exercises as a caring leader is to thank those who courageously speak up. This is his way of validating that their voices matter.

Larry Sutton, founder and president of RNR Tire Express, explained how he invites anyone sitting around the table with him to point out his communication fumbles. Larry has on more than one occasion told his team, "I'm going to say something stupid, or I'm going to have the wrong idea, and what I expect from you is to stand up and slap the crap out of me and tell me I'm wrong. Not sit back and tell me how I'm right." Larry's invitation to his people to honestly speak up is refreshing and is also a requirement for the caring leader who wants to create a safe space in which others can grow.

I recall leading a diversity and inclusion council some years back. In the room, there were Latinx, African Americans, those from the LGBTQ community, and more. My manager asked me to lead that group, I think, because I am open-minded and I bring people together. I saw my role as the one who allowed space for all voices while also ensuring a high level of respectful conversations. Whenever I felt that one set of voices was taking over the discussion, I would adjust my positioning in the room as if to physically open space, and then I would either mention what another person said to take the discussion down a different path or ask a person by name what his or her thoughts were on that or a different topic.

This process was and still is very important to me. If all voices are not heard, then the people in the room, on the team, and in the organization miss a huge opportunity to improve employee experience and that feeling of safety. It is both the invitation to speak and the validation that you heard them that makes all the difference in helping people to feel safe.

Hearing critical feedback, as Larry alluded to, can be difficult. None-theless, caring leaders show an openness to hear the hard things, which creates a safe space for innovation and business success.

Show an Openness to Hear the Hard Things

As in my conversation with Larry, Phil Burgess, chief people and opera-tions officer at C Space, demonstrated the openness to hear and process hard things. Leaders often feel fearful of what they might hear from those they lead, but the caring leader does as Phil described to me and walks directly into the feedback:

> I focus a lot on trying to provide space for people to point out where I'm getting stuff wrong. And then I try to be as vocal as I can with my team about, "Yeah, this is some of the feedback you gave me about how I'm not running team meetings quite as effectively as you want, and we're going to try something differ-ent today." And I think that that helps give me confidence, and it'll help them to give me feedback on what I'm getting right, which builds my own confidence and self-esteem as a leader, and it also helps them not . . . see me just as the guy that's got all the answers, but as someone who's . . . working with them.

I remember how quiet a room can get when the executives show up to a meeting. No one wants to speak unless spoken to.

Nick Smarrelli, CEO of GadellNet Consulting Services, seems to find comfort in the fact that those he leads openly speak out against some-thing he might say or do. Here is how he described that environment:

> I'm really happy to be in a culture of acceptance; we have a cul-ture that even though given my title, I have an entire organiza-tion, whatever layer they are in that organization, that is willing to call me out. . . . Some people do it with a sense of humor, some people do it with a sense of directness, but regardless, we've created a culture that it's OK to tell the CEO, "You're not acting in accordance to the best version of yourself." My responsibility

in hearing that is to acknowledge it and say, "I am not, and I apologize for that."

I think that these leaders are courageous and set themselves apart from many other leaders in their desire to hear and handle the hard truth. That receptivity creates a safe environment in which others can flourish. Whether they know it or not, they are also modeling psychological safety.

Foster Psychological Safety

In her book *The Fearless Organization: Creating Psychological Safety in the Workplace for Learning, Innovation, and Growth*, Amy C. Edmondson summarizes a psychologically safe workplace as

> a climate in which people are comfortable expressing and being themselves. More specifically, they feel comfortable sharing concerns and mistakes without fear of embarrassment or retribution. They are confident that they can speak up, and won't be humiliated, ignored, or blamed. They know they can ask questions when they are unsure about something.[2]

For the caring leader, creating a psychologically safe workplace goes hand in hand with showing concern and kindness for those we lead. For any of the behaviors in this book to take hold, and for us to achieve any level of leadership success, we must make sure that our people feel truly safe.

Organizational leaders who want more innovation and problem-solving curate safe spaces by fostering psychological safety. They create this muscle by practicing it, as we cannot create this type of environment overnight.

Practice Psychologically Safe Interactions

Peter Melby, CEO of Greystone Technology, has spent the last several years building a culture that allows everyone to practice what psychologically safe interactions look like. What the leaders at Greystone realized was that to build a culture where people are transparent and feel safe to admit they don't know something, you have to "celebrate together and just show up as a real person, not someone who's defensive or just trying to show the best side of what's happening. That doesn't happen overnight, and it only happens when there's consistent practice."

To create the space for practice, Peter and his team created a straightforward system to cover the gray areas of manager and employee interactions. What does this system look like? Managers have two monthly meetings with their people; one of the meetings is one-on-one and the other is a team meeting. At each meeting, the manager and team member use a specific set of questions that allow them to practice getting to know where everyone is at. Additionally, their performance management process requires a monthly one-on-one with the manager to gauge success and areas to work on.

Peter mentioned that he and his team put some structure to conversations, because they don't happen naturally, as most avoid them out of discomfort. When reflecting on this practice, Peter said, "By doing that, in a monthly cadence, we practice it to the point that . . . the humanity becomes very normal, and psychological safety becomes something that's significantly more possible to achieve than if we just left everybody to their own devices."

Another way to create a safe space for those who look to you for guidance is to do as Andy Boian, founder and CEO of Dovetail Solutions, does in that he speaks last at any meeting. Of this practice, here is Andy's reflection:

> Let's say we have a strategy meeting on a topic or we're dealing with a difficult client, and we all have come together as a team to talk about how to manage this situation. If I speak first, it defeats the purpose. I speak last for two reasons: One, I gain people's perspective without having to say anything, so people get to voice what they want to voice. They feel comfortable without any caveats saying what they want to say, and I get the benefit of listening to that, before I speak, which is enormously helpful all

the time, even if I don't necessarily agree or if I think something different, or it goes long; I still listen. . . . Second . . . I think when it is my turn to speak, I want to speak with everybody's thoughts in mind. If I come in with an agenda, I'm not leading.

This line of thinking came up many times in my interviews. I think it is brilliant to practice working in a safe environment. I also think it's very emotionally intelligent to listen first and allow others to speak. This is one of the reasons why caring leadership is an art form. It takes consistent practice.

Here are some additional things to consider if you want to create psychological safety for your teams and your organization as a whole. Maybe you can practice these too!

Acknowledge When Your Employees Speak Up

When you're in a group meeting and somebody at the table expresses an opinion that differs from the dominant narrative in the room, take the time not only to acknowledge that person's perspective but also to *listen* to what she has to say—especially if she indicates that your organization is not on the right path.

If you don't allow for *all* voices within your organization to be heard, but only the obvious ones, those with countering views won't feel safe because they will know that your organization is not inclusive of someone like them.

Invite People to Speak Up

One thing you can do as a leader to create a sense of psychological safety is to invite feedback—and be open to all the feedback you receive, even if it makes you uncomfortable or reflects changes that you, personally, need to make. This is what Mark Nagel, quoted earlier in the chapter, illustrated when he asked for opinions of those around the table.

Remember, there *is* no perfect leader, and while no leader seeks out or welcomes mistakes, inviting your employees to be honest about their thoughts and fears and hopes, and encouraging them to speak up when they see or hear something that needs to change, can help you improve your approach as an individual and as an organization. A finer point to mention is that we also show care when we guide our people on when, exactly, it is appropriate to speak our minds. If we speak so openly that we dissuade others from speaking or we are too direct at the wrong time, we don't do ourselves justice. It's just as important that the caring leader provide direction on timing of feedback as it is to provide the space for it.

By offering a clear invitation for your employees to speak up, and by creating boundaries around how and when they should feel free to speak up, you can help direct employee feedback in the most beneficial and valuable way. It is equally important to be more inclusive in your invitations to speak up.

Expand Your Invitation to Speak

It's important to consider whom you are inviting to speak up. Have you invited the appropriate people to the conversation? Are you being inclusive of all perspectives? Who is seated at the table? Who is not in the room that perhaps should be? When you are thinking about how to create psychological safety for your employees, you *have* to ask yourself, "How much more inclusive can I be?"

Are you inviting people who identify in different ways, or who perhaps don't share the same experiences or perspectives as other people in the room? How are you giving them the opportunity to share their feedback on a specific issue or initiative?

For marginalized groups in the workforce, feeling safe, feeling included, and feeling that their voice matters is even trickier. Without realizing it, many leaders allow those who look to them for safety and guidance to feel unsafe because of microaggressions that the employees experience every day. Managers need to understand the meaning and impact of these microaggressions in order to evolve into caring and effective leaders.

Protect Those You Lead from Microaggressions

Microaggression was coined in the 1970s by Chester M. Pierce, MD, a Harvard psychiatrist. Today's definition can be credited to Derald Wing Sue, a professor of counseling psychology at Columbia University. Sue defines microaggressions in this way:

> Microaggressions are the brief and commonplace daily verbal, behavioral, and environmental indignities, whether intentional or unintentional, that communicate hostile, derogatory, or negative racial, gender, sexual-orientation, and religious slights and insults to the target person or group.[3]

Some examples of microaggressions are:

- A White woman clutching her purse when entering an elevator with a Black man

- A White person asking to touch a Black person's hair

- Someone volunteering one of their Asian colleagues to bring fried rice to a company picnic

T. Renata Robinson, PhD, chief human resources officer at Colorado Coalition for the Homeless and a diversity and inclusion expert, provided more examples of microaggressions toward African American people:

- Someone says to a Black woman, "You are really pretty!" Then, after getting to know her a bit more, the person says, "Oh my gosh, you are so smart too!" This assumes that a Black woman cannot be both pretty and smart.

- A White man tries to speak for a person of color in a meeting: "What she is trying to say is . . ." This presumes that she cannot communicate on her own.

- When a Black person is articulate, a White person says, "Oh my gosh, you articulate so well!" This presumes that anyone else who looks like this individual doesn't speak in an articulate manner.

Jennifer Fairweather, director of human resources for Jefferson County, Colorado, shared with me what she put in place to protect employees from microaggressions in their workplace. The first step was a meeting of the minds around how to show up in the workplace. About this issue she shared, "Those expectations include respect, appreciating differences, and valuing inclusivity." Admittedly, she knows that verbal buy-in is not always in line with actions. She explained, "What we found is that when they were occurring, people were not speaking up. Rather, they let the issues fester to a point where people harbored ill will; they wanted to resign or were looking for someone to fix the problem."

Jennifer worked with her team to come up with objectives to ensure that individuals directly addressed microaggressions. Jennifer shared that they utilize their internal training department to help them meet these learning objectives, and occasionally they enlist an outside mediator if needed.

When Microaggressions Turn from Hurt to Enlightenment

The most compelling part of my interviews on my podcast is when I ask the leaders to describe a time when they were not the best version of themselves. I can think of three times when the stories left me with my jaw wide open. The admission of Cori Burbach, assistant city manager for the City of Dubuque, to a microaggression was on the top of the list. Cori and other organizational leaders embarked on work around microaggressions as a part of their efforts of creating a more diverse workforce, given their mostly White community.

While at a leadership team book club meeting, Cori found herself guilty of a microaggression toward someone she greatly respected. Cori explained what happened:

> We were breaking into small groups and talking about a book that was very rooted in a lot of issues around race and Black and White. . . . I noticed that we had three of our Black employees that were all going to one group. So, the group that I was in was

not going to have that perspective, and a couple of us really wanted to have that perspective. . . . So, I leaned over to one of my Black male colleagues, who I value very much in a personal relationship, and I looked at him and I said, "Would you please be the token Black man in this conversation?" And the minute I said it, I regretted it! I thought, "Crap!" And I thought, now if I draw attention to it, it's going to make it worse. So, we moved on, and I'm so grateful for this man in my life. He came up to me afterward and he said, "I didn't know what to do when you said that to me. . . . We talk all the time about intent versus impact . . . I know your intent wasn't bad, but the impact was. All of a sudden, I felt completely singled out. I felt like I didn't know how to address it. I felt like nobody else in the room stood up for me."

Cori said that she met with him a couple of times after that incident, and he "gave me the grace" to apologize and to understand what it meant for him. Their relationship was restored, and they both nervously presented this story to the leadership team. Since then, as a team, they have been having conversations and doing interactive exercises to bring these discussions to the surface. In hindsight, Cori could have organized the book club into diverse groups ahead of time to ensure that each group was more representative of the topic. This would have prevented the need for this interaction in the first place.

Cori's big awakening was learning that her colleague who was on the receiving end of this microaggression had physical symptoms and could not concentrate for the rest of the day after the interaction. Others on the leadership team also shared their physical responses to these types of exchanges.

Cori is a caring leader because she recognized what she did, met her colleague where he was, and took time to understand the impact of her actions. She could have brushed the entire thing under the carpet. Instead, she met that feedback head-on, never minimized the role she played, and used her learning to help others. Caring leaders are not perfect, but they are more self-aware and do not have an issue with admitting their mistakes.

My Experience with Microaggressions

As a biracial woman who presents as a black woman, I also have experienced the sting of microaggressions. I have ignored many microaggressions, as I realize that many are founded in ignorance. There have been times when I attempted to educate someone when the person told me my skin is so pretty because "it is lighter than the others'!" Mostly, I just let the microaggressions roll off my shoulders.

I have had many diverse people on my teams over the years. When people make comments about someone's health issues, language differences, or cultural background, as a manager, I do not sit and tolerate it. If I were to do that, then I would be complicit in the microaggressions. Instead, the lawyer in me seeks to defend and advocate. Knowing what I know about human nature, though, I do not act aggressively in my advocacy: first, because I do not want to advance the inaccurate stereotypes of people who look like me; second, I know that someone is always watching. I want to model the right responses for others to follow.

Here are ways I approach microaggressions, whether they are against me or a team member:

1. I ask the person why he said what he said. I do this because often people make inaccurate assumptions based upon their past consumption of bad information. Because I assume this, I don't need to go at it aggressively but more to seek to understand their thinking.

2. I show the person that I am actively listening to what he says by leaning in, shaking my head, and even repeating back what I heard to make sure I understand his thinking.

3. Then, I meet him where he is and let him know where I can see his thinking and, if applicable, where I might agree with him.

4. Next, I ask permission to share why I think his statement is not quite accurate. I try to use as much factual and historical language as I can. Sometimes this is easier than at other times, and emotions come out too.

5. If it was a microaggression against someone else, I might end with a question like "Can you see now how what you said offended (or hurt) so and so?" Either way, I let the person know that I will not accept this type of treatment and that I would also defend him as well if someone were to treat him this way.

Creating safe spaces for those we lead is imperative if we want them to want to stay with us longer, innovate, go over and above for the team, and exceed customer expectations. Acknowledging and then protecting those we lead from microaggressions is one way to create safe spaces. If employees don't feel safe, they will not feel loyal or committed to team and organizational success.

The Art of Caring Leadership in Practice

We all want to feel safe at work—emotionally, physically, and mentally. Create an environment that allows opinions and ideas to be heard in a nonthreatening way. When we help those we lead to feel safe, they are freed up to be their best unique selves for the team and the organization. Commit today to clear away any norms that get in the way of offering this gift to your team.

Caring Leader Highlight

Kevin Patterson
chief executive officer, Connect for Health Colorado

- **Interviewed on:** Episode 113, "Leaders with Heart Set a Clear Vision for Others to Follow"

- **Aha moment:** Years before he was CEO of Connect for Health Colorado, Kevin started out teaching English to seventh graders on the north side of Houston. As he described, "That's a tough age to deal with, and getting them to care about punctuation was quite the task." Though it was a completely different working environment with its own set of unique challenges, Kevin said, it gave him practical skills for providing a safe space where people could thrive in their own way. He continued, "It really prepared me for a lot of the ways that I have engaged in the workplace going forward. Again, asking a lot of questions, being able to explain things in a number of different fashions, because you understand that people learn in different modes." Whether Kevin was leading a classroom of seventh graders or is leading more than a hundred employees across his organization, the same principles of psychological safety apply. He knows that people need to feel trusted, supported, and included to turn in their best work, and that the responsibility of fostering that kind of environment invariably falls to the caring leader.

- **How they embody caring leadership:** Creating safe spaces for your employees looks like a lot of different things depending on your specific career, as this chapter established. But certain things hold true across the board, and Kevin's leadership principles are very much in line with those values. "I try to be very communicative and clear about expectations. I try my best not to micromanage," he said. "If you're very clear about where you want them to end up by when, you don't have to tell them to make three left turns to end up in the same place." Extending that level of trust to your employees is exactly the kind of behavior that makes them feel safe to be their best self.

- **Guiding philosophy:**

  - *Leaders must provide a clear vision and direction to help those who follow them, but they shouldn't dictate every detail.* As Kevin said before, micromanaging can kill any sense of safety at work, since it communicates the impression that you don't trust employees' instincts. Provide a direction to pursue and an objective to achieve, but be open to other ways of getting there. The topic of empowering employees by setting a clear direction is discussed in chapter 8 in more detail.

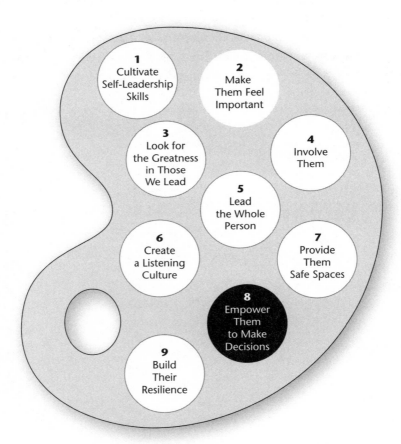

The Caring Leadership Framework

8

Empower Them to Make Decisions

• • •

You've got to be able to trust the wisdom of the team.
Jandel Allen-Davis, MD, president and CEO, Craig Hospital

One of the most crippling things managers do to those they lead is micromanage their every move, making it difficult for their employees to think and act independently. Caring leaders trade micromanagement for empowerment, by allowing those they lead room to do what they think is right even if that means making a mistake. These leaders understand that true growth and learning comes through empowerment and that those they lead are adults who can make their own decisions. The caring leader is secure and self-confident enough to entrust others with this autonomy; in contrast, consider the insecure leader, who feels every task must be tightly controlled to ensure that his or her vision is fulfilled.

I remember working for a manager who wanted to know my every move and how I planned to go about achieving a project she put in my lap. She required that I meet with her every week on the timeline for completion, and then she brought one of her colleagues in to "work with" me without my asking. I have an entrepreneurial spirit. So, this immediately felt like she was squeezing me. What should my manager have done? She should have allowed me to accomplish that project, using my experience and insight, and met with me weekly to see how things were progressing. At those weekly check-ins, she could have asked if I needed any assistance. Instead, I felt a total lack of respect and trust. Therefore, I quickly looked for an exit strategy from her team and that organization.

Provide Fertile Soil

I was very taken by the imagery of the words that Christinne Johnson of FirstBank used to describe how she sees her role in empowerment: "I try to clear the path and encourage the heart and then get out of the way, because people want to . . . excel and they want to be empowered, and they want to . . . do these great things. And the last thing I want to do is be in the way of that. So, that's exactly what I try to do—open up the paths, open up the doors." I have worked with Christinne, and I have seen how she empowers the other leaders who report to her.

Mareo McCracken, chief customer officer at Movemedical, presented a pragmatic and compelling look at the role of empowerment:

> Because often when you're not in a leadership role, you feel like you don't have control over the things you want to do. So, you think you'll get more control by being a leader, but what I've learned is that leaders often have less actual control because they're reliant. You have to rely so much on the people you lead that there's even less that you have the ability to actually do yourself. If you can't learn to delegate and empower, you can't really be a leader.

Mareo was spot-on! If you are not empowering others to make their own decisions and do their best work, you are not a caring leader.

One of the ways to show those you lead that you care is to loosen up control, be clear on your expectations, and trust them to do what you hired them to do. Keith Freier, director of operational systems and technology at Pacific Northwest National Laboratory, shared his unique way of looking at clearing the path:

> Somebody along the way told me . . . your job as a leader is to build the runway and then get out of the way and let them fly and land the planes. And it's a simple analogy, but it makes a lot of sense . . . that we as leaders oftentimes might get too tied up in the day-to-day details and micromanage. The best thing is to select a very highly qualified team, set your expectations,

and then fully empower them to be successful and get out of their way. And let them know that you're here to support them.

You will notice that I am not referring to *delegation* but *empowerment*. To *delegate* is to ask someone to perform an act in the place of another.[1] Empowerment is more expansive. Merriam-Webster defines *empower* as "to promote the self-actualization or influence of."[2] I prefer to empower, because I want those I lead to step outside of expected parameters not only to solve business challenges but also to use their gifts to the highest purpose for themselves and the team. This is the difference that makes all the difference for those led by caring leaders. It's not just "Go do this thing for me, please, since I am unable to do it"; it adds, "Do what is necessary to achieve the ends we both understand, and do it with creativity and gusto!"

To truly empower those we lead, we do need to set clear expectations of team and organizational goals and include the team in deciding what the team's goal and objectives should be.

Set Clear Expectations

Caring leaders set clear expectations for those they lead so that they do not cause confusion and frustration. When employees derive a sense of accomplishment from achieving what they set out to do, they have a deep connection to their work. The clearer that employees are about what is expected of them, the more they feel that the work they do is meaningful. Meaningful work is a primary driver of employee loyalty.

As Cheryl Fullerton, executive vice president, people and communications, at Corus Entertainment, so intelligently put it, "The most important thing I think a leader is there to do is be very clear about objectives, and make sure . . . people know why and how they fit into what great looks like. . . . Great people will sometimes just figure out all the rest on their own."

Melissa Eovine, manager of sponsorship at the Fellowship of Catholic University Students (FOCUS), added some rich texture to Cheryl's thoughts in pointing out that there is a balance between empowerment and clarity: "The more specific detail you can give them with the freedom to do it in the way that they need, is more than efficient. Because if there is something that needs to be done and they're creative in the way that they do it, then you're allowing both to happen."

Speaking in our interview about what caring for those we lead means, Kevin Patterson said, "I think it's really important in an organization that everybody's really clear . . . get everybody on the same page . . . and then . . . the song sounds right. If you're on a different page, everybody's not singing the same song. . . . It doesn't sound right."

Kevin highlighted that it is clarity that turns empowerment into a gift. Without it, team members are left feeling disoriented and doubtful about their course of action. As he pointed out, once they are clear on the direction, it is less important that they get there the way we want them to. They need to figure out their own path. They will feel more accomplished if they get there on their own.

Rich Gassen of the University of Wisconsin–Madison understood this concept when he took it upon himself to rewrite the mission and strategic vision for his small department, and he worked with his team to come up with the goals for their unit. To make the goals front and center in their daily operations, they print them out on large-format signs and post them where everyone can see them. He uses that mission and vision as a guiding star when meeting with team members, and he refers back to them when working to brainstorm with his team and when administering performance reviews.

When used in this way, mission, values, and goals come to life and provide the clarity needed to ensure that everyone is on the same page, best prepared to thrive, and hearing the same song.

When we think of the caring leader, we must realize that there is a balance between giving clear direction and leading with heart. If we are too loose in our direction, then team members might feel insecure and a little lost; when we are clear with them, as Kevin highlighted above, we help to cure those insecurities and embolden our people. Clarity is an important brushstroke for the caring leader. This is a special combination.

The leader who can set a clear path while also demonstrating concern and compassion for how her people walk the path has the special touch of a caring leader. Another special hue in the caring leader's palette is when she invites risk-taking as part of innovating and helping people grow.

Invite Risk-Taking

Risk-taking goes hand in hand with empowerment. Why do I think that? The definition of *empowerment* is "the granting of the power, right, or authority to perform various acts or duties."[3] Implicit in empowerment is a level of independence or minimal oversight. Mistakes happen whether or not someone is watching.

Many employees are fearful of making mistakes because of the potential ramifications, based upon their personal experiences. Those who lead with heart invite risk-taking and allow thoughtful mistakes. As a result, team members who report to this type of leader are more likely to innovate and collaborate to overcome business challenges, since they feel free to do so. Micromanagement is the enemy of these efforts.

When encouraging his teachers to take risks, Andrew McDonald, principal of Our Lady of Loreto Catholic School, invites them to be reflective both when something works and when it doesn't. When something does not work, Andrew coaches his teachers to ask, "What could I have done differently?" or "Where might we have gone off track?"

Andrew's point about the importance of debriefing after taking risks or embarking on a new process or project is a good one. It not only allows for reflection and learning but also acts as an accountability source for all involved.

Jo-Ann Robertson, CEO of Ketchum London, has a refreshing perspective on risk-taking: "If they take the initiative and they're entrepreneurial, and it goes wrong . . . I'll be there to have their back and help them to learn from it. . . . But let's take those learnings and build from it. I'll help you put it back together and move forward."

Both Andrew's and Jo-Ann's mindsets also reinforce the psychological safety concept discussed in chapter 7. The caring leader wants to see and unleash the best ideas from his people. To do this, he understands that removing barriers to innovative thinking, such as fear of mistakes or being ridiculed for voicing opinions, is the only way to reveal those ideas.

Although caring leaders empower their people to take risks and let them arrive at their own conclusions in their own way, they are still a resource for their people when they need guidance or direction.

Be a Resource

There is a difference between empowering people and abdicating your responsibility. We can observe that caring leaders empower those they lead by allowing them to be courageous to move the business forward in responsible ways. Then the leader stands as a resource or as a sounding board. The leader might check in with his team member or just be in the distance ready to help.

Many years ago, as a part of our honeymoon, my husband and I went to a five-star restaurant. It was lovely! I recall that they introduced five different servers for our table, but we saw them only when they sensed that we needed them. They remained in the shadows. When our glasses were empty or we needed more bread, one of those servers would just appear. This is what I have in mind when I think of the caring leader who empowers her team. Once she allows that freedom, she is just a resource for her team when they need help or more direction.

In alignment with that concept, D'anthony Tillery, assistant vice president of talent acquisition at Atrium Health, explained, "You have to really give the employees the right level of support and freedom to make the right decisions. . . . You also have to give them the guide rails to ensure that they understand. Given that power, they also have an opportunity to engage with you, ensuring that they are pointing toward the right direction."

Steve McIntosh, founder and CEO of CML Offshore Recruitment, sees empowerment as a partnership between the team member and the organization: "My approach to leadership these days is not to tell people what to do, but to agree what needs to be done, and to make sure they have the resources and the support they need to be able to do it well."

Greg Wathen, president and CEO of the Economic Development Coalition of Southwest Indiana, views empowerment as a form of respect between individuals. In his view, how one achieves a goal or objective is less important. His philosophy is to respect that everyone brings different styles and skills to the table. Greg's focus is on being collaborative and understanding. I know this to be true about Greg because I met him after seeing a post on social media by one of his colleagues. This female executive, who was subordinate to Greg, needed to go into a meeting, but she had her child at work with her. What stood out about Greg as a CEO was that he waited outside the meeting and cared for her child while she led the meeting inside. That is collaboration and understanding at its best!

Chuck Runyon, of Anytime Fitness, believes that empowerment is just his way of building up those he leads, and then they build up the business in return: "So, every day . . . we drive to work thinking we work for these people. They don't work for us. . . . It's our job to make sure they have the capabilities, they have the resources, they have the right plan. A lot of times, they're creating the plan, and we're just helping them edit it or prioritize a plan and they need a sounding board."

You can easily see how leaders who care think of empowerment differently. Yet, they all create a fertile ground on which those they lead can do their best work with limited constraints. These leaders look at risk-taking as part of standard operating procedures for the workplace, but they do not abandon their people in the process. They all show us that caring leadership is, indeed, an art form.

The Art of Caring Leadership in Practice

Don't think of empowerment as giving up control. Think of it as allowing those you lead to show themselves and you that they can achieve great things with little oversight. Sit with your people and talk to them about projects that they can lead without you. Set out to let them know you trust them to do good work for the team.

Caring Leader Highlight

Larry Sutton
founder and president, RNR Tire Express

- **Interviewed on:** Episode 70, "Leaders with Heart Empower Their People to Do Their Best Work"

- **Industry/specialization:** Automotive (tire/retail)

- **Aha moment:** After being fortunate enough to franchise his business, Larry saw new levels of success in his professional life. He believed that he had to maintain complete control to keep this early momentum going, so he bore the brunt of the entire company's workload. Soon enough, his business partner sat him down and told him that he couldn't keep micromanaging every operation and every franchise, and that his overbearing leadership made some of his employees feel disempowered. "Realizing that I haven't empowered anybody, but was just over-lording and micromanaging, was a big awakening for me," Larry professed. From then on, Larry delegated some of his responsibilities and became focused on empowering his workforce to make decisions for themselves and speak up when they disagreed with him.

- **How they embody caring leadership:** In many ways, Larry's journey parallels the transition from an insecure leader to a caring one. The insecure leader feels every task must be tightly controlled to ensure that his vision is fulfilled, whereas the caring leader is confident enough to entrust others with this autonomy. Larry knows that employees need to make their own decisions, take charge for themselves, and have their own voice. "They are not truly empowered if that's not the case," he suggested. "If they're not empowered, they won't grow to be the best they can be. . . . If they don't have the freedom to disagree, their empowerment will start chipping away."

- **Guiding philosophy:**

  - **Your way is not the only way.** It may not even be the best way. If you've truly done your job as a caring leader, you will have assembled a team of employees that collectively is as capable as you are (if not more so). Learn to lean on your team and take advantage of their unique approaches to problem-solving. Surrender your ego and allow other people into the decision-making process. Trust them as they trust you.

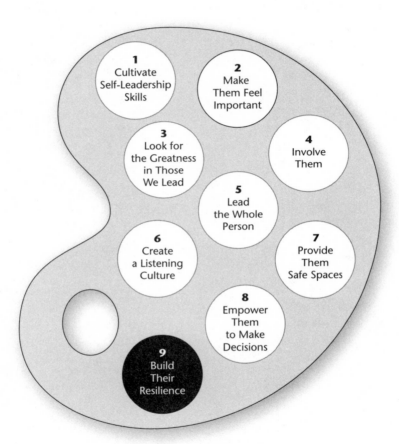

The Caring Leadership Framework

9

Build Their Resilience

• • •

If I wasn't in pain, then I would not have done certain things.
Pain brings together a lot of great people and opportunities.
Kristy McCann Flynn, cofounder and CEO, GoCoach

Inside and outside the workplace, obstacles and challenges are all around. Caring leaders focus on building resilience within those they lead to help them respond to inevitable adversity and bounce back to become stronger. This involves helping them reframe their current circumstances, learn from what is happening around them, and see the challenges and obstacles in their paths as opportunities to grow and progress in their careers and connect more deeply.

As I write this, we are in the middle of a global pandemic. There is no more important time in history for leaders to step up and help build a more resilient world. *Resilience* is "an ability to recover from or adjust easily to misfortune or change.[1] The key to resilience is that we must face some type of challenge, obstacle, or adversity in order to need it. In other words, we need challenges to grow our resilience muscle.

Why should leaders need to help build the resilience of those they lead? The more quickly those you lead bounce back from challenges, the more quickly they can return to meaningful work that drives teams and organizations forward.

My Story of Resilience

As I alluded to in the introduction to this book, I had my share of adversity as a child. I will describe here how one path of rejection made me develop the skill of resilience. My biracial and interfaith background made for an interesting and challenging childhood.

My mom's parents loved me, but they were ashamed of my parents' union, of which I was a constant reminder. As a result, I was never invited to public family gatherings, and no pictures of me hung in my grandmother's home. I was an outsider, and there was no hiding it. The first time I attended a large family gathering, it was my grandmother's funeral. I was thirty-six years old. That was a surreal experience, and it was the first time that no one excluded me from attending.

This journey of rejection left me feeling not good enough, unheard, and unimportant. I had a choice. I could live my life wallowing in my past, or I could use my past as the fuel I needed to exercise my hard-earned resilience muscle and help others do the same. I chose the latter. There are many benefits of growing up in a biracial and interfaith family. The biggest benefit is my ability to see all sides of one story. I can remain both objective and compassionate. Having said that, I fall into victim thinking occasionally and need help to get out. Those we lead need that same help. Often, they just need someone to be their guide through what can often be the landmines of life.

Be Their Guide

Often when employees are facing difficult times, they may not feel that they can come to those whom they think of as their manager or boss. The key here is to be an open sounding board who can present a different way of thinking about the employees' current circumstances.

Jim Reuter, president and CEO of FirstBank, recalled some instances when employees came to him with tough experiences in their lives. Jim sees these interactions as a compliment, because "that wouldn't happen if they didn't feel like I was someone they could trust and then someone they thought could help them through that."

Some years ago, my daughter was struggling with an unhealthy friendship. She had a sense that she was being used, but she did not know how to approach her friend. After she spent a couple of weeks fretting over what might happen to her reputation if she confronted this friend, I spoke with her about her options. I helped her remain unemotional as she thought through her approach, and then she felt more confident. While she was never really close again with that young lady, my daughter realized that this was the best result for her sanity. I served as her guide when she felt lost.

We all face challenges. I know very few people who can claim that they have never had some type of adversity in their life. Being there to help them recalibrate their thinking is another way to show them that you care. Don Davis, county manager of Jefferson County, Colorado, and a former military leader, explained it this way:

> Back in my days in the military, we used compasses for land navigation. We have to have an azimuth, which is a general direction that you follow in order to get to your destination. When you come upon obstacles, like a river or a lake, you point the compass across that obstacle. Then, you find the reference point. Afterwards, you put the compass in your pocket; then you maneuver and walk around the obstacle. Next, you get back on your reference point, and then you take the compass out of your pocket. Lastly, you get back on your azimuth. Vision helps you in the good times and in the bad. You could get blinded by the peaks of success, or you could get lost in the valley of despair and troubles. But, you need to have a vision to direct you.

What I love about Don's explanation is that we, as leaders, can be the azimuth for those we lead. I remember being that for one of my team members, who was nervous about doing a presentation for a group of executives. To help her get over her nervousness, I helped her think differently about those to whom she was presenting. I told her that they took their pants off one leg at a time like the rest of us. By helping her see how they were human and nothing to be afraid of, she was no longer afraid, and she won that business after that presentation! I chose to be her guide to get her back to her best self.

Leaders must help those they lead create their vision for the future. With their special blend of leadership, caring leaders go out of their way to help their people get back on course despite barriers and obstacles in their path. They are both guides and azimuths.

Help Them Find Courage

I had a very strange relationship with my maternal grandmother. On one hand, she loved me and was my biggest cheerleader. On the other hand, she felt compelled to keep me hidden from those in her community. To this day, it hurts me to write this. Nonetheless, in many ways, she helped me find the courage to overcome fear and to stay strong when faced with obstacles in my life.

I built a lot of resilience from the rejection and issues with my family, and the same person who brought on those struggles always taught me, "Never let them see you sweat" and "Keep your chin up." By doing that, she showed me that she cared for me. It is much as Mareo McCracken, chief customer officer at Movemedical, described how he sees his role for those he leads:

> But what I do believe is encouraging people and giving people courage because courage is the ability to take action in the face of fear, grief, or pain. And everything that stops us in life is either something we're afraid of . . . we have a painful experience from . . . or there's some kind of sadness or grief. . . . One of those reasons stops us from taking the right action. It could be fear of action; it could be fear of the results of that action. There are so many different types of fear. But I think if, as a leader, I can

possibly help someone have enough courage to take one step to just do something that they're not doing today, then that's my main focus and my main job.

I have heard that leaders wear the hat of therapist often. While we cannot formally claim that title, there are many times, especially during crises in our organizations and with our teams, when leaders must show up with the greatest empathy, care, and concern. Nonetheless, leaders are not perfect.

During my interviews, I asked all of the leaders about a time when they were not the best version of themselves and what they did to come out of it. Those in the following examples, like many of those I interviewed, started off in a rocky place but had an awakening that allowed them to help others become more resilient.

Benilda Samuels, vice president of programs, Rose Family Foundation, shared a rich story about when she worked for a city human services agency as its public affairs officer. Over the two and a half years that she worked in that role, sixteen children died in foster care. She recalled never pausing or allowing others to pause through that rough time. Admittedly, she allowed her emotions of fear and sadness to get the best of her, and they spilled over to those who looked to her for leadership. This experience made her reflect on how she could have "brought people in and held them closer" to get the team through that time with less heartache.

Some years later, Benilda had the opportunity to use her past challenges with the human services role to assist the founder at the next organization where she worked. His organization was founded on an evidence-based model that was supposed to help women and children. Because of this, the model was always tested by outside agencies. A foreign government reviewed the model and found that it did not have an effect on the lives of women and children. This left the founder very distressed because it was his life's work.

Benilda recalled going to dinner with the founder before the article regarding this government's findings came out. In that moment, recalling her human services experience, Benilda felt equipped to speak to him. She felt that she could help bring down the stress level for him. She said that she produced an annual calendar that for each month displayed a picture of a baby who had been positively impacted by the program and model. Benilda recalled that she took that calendar and handed it to her CEO and said, "No matter what happens tomorrow and what they say, I want you to remember, I want you to look at these twelve children and know that you have made their lives better. And I want you to know that there's thousands of children who you've made their lives better, because you had the vision for something like this."

As her CEO went into an interview that was in response to the article, she continued to reassure him of his positive impact. Of that interaction, Benilda exclaimed, "And you could just see him sort of take a breath, being able to reflect back and say to himself, this is true!"

I adore this story because it illustrates what Scott Shay, cofounder and chairman of Signature Bank, declared in a clear and compelling way: "Sometimes, it is in our most intimate encounters that we recognize things that have epic consequences in our life." For Benilda, her traumatic experience working in that human services agency through that crisis helped her to realize that she possessed the power to help others reframe their challenges. She found that strength through her own adversity. Moreover, she helped her CEO to find courage to deal with what was in front of him.

Aaron Skogen, general manager of Aquatix by Landscape Structures, Inc., bravely shared a time when he was focused on the negative environment in his organization and failed to be there for his team. The organization that Aaron was working for was going through a tough time. Instead of standing closer to his team, he went silent. He recalled that doing so "accentuated the tension within the organization" because he was not visible or transparent. This was a huge learning experience for Aaron, as his team needed him to be there. They wanted his help to find the courage to get through this tough time. After that experience, Aaron focused on walking around and touching base with his people, many of whom asked where he had been. Aaron humbly admitted to them that he had lost his way and how important it was for him to be with them and communicating with them.

The learning from Aaron's experience is that those we lead will watch how we handle adversity and might begin to model it. Additionally, we help our team members overcome challenges not by doing it by ourselves in some closet but by being there for one another. Caring leaders are not perfect, but their heart is, like Aaron's, front and center of how they show up.

Make It a Team Effort

Just as the first chapter discussed how the leader must have a support system to help her reframe circumstances and to believe in her, so too must those we lead have a team of supporters. The leader is the one who must corral the larger team together to work to overcome challenges. This does not always happen naturally, but the caring leader knows that it takes a village.

Alex Smith, chief human resources officer and chief change officer for the City of Memphis, described this team approach as "a focus of collaboration and trust and really a codependency with each other where no one feels like they are isolated on an island by themselves. We all feel that we are in it together, and I think that is important and that all of us achieve and succeed together, and we also face challenges and failures together. And we solve them together and work through those things together."

This is a refreshing and freeing approach for the leader, because she does not have to try to be the superhero and solve her team members' issues on her own. If the leader does her job, by building trust inside the team and between team members, then it is not a stretch to access the team's power to help one another overcome challenges. You can see how this would uplift the team and the organization.

Shawnté Cox Holland, head of culture and engagement at Vanguard, described how to build adversity-withstanding trust: "It's really important to allow people to get to know you better, to be humble and vulnerable with your team and to be human, so that people realize that people will make mistakes, and that's OK. What matters is how we recover from them, how we come together as a team to work on something."

I liken becoming more resilient to building muscle. We cannot tone and strengthen our arms without some sort of strength training. Building muscle basically tears it before it grows. It is some really hard work, and if it's done right, we sweat a lot and it hurts like heck! This is how building resilience works. The more adversity we face and challenges we overcome, the more our resilience muscle grows. We should see any obstacle, challenge, crisis, or adversity as an opportunity to build that muscle. Leaders must help their own people do the same.

Below are a few ways to use challenging circumstances to help build resilience muscle in us and those we lead:

- Don't run away. Our natural inclination is to run away from things that frighten us or challenge the status quo. This is like giving up in the middle of a workout or marathon. We will not get to the end or obtain the results we want unless we finish and hit the lofty goal head-on. I don't mean that we shouldn't take precautions to protect ourselves. Instead, do that, and continue to show up and stand firm as our best that day. This act alone helps us build resilience in ourselves and those we lead.

- See the bright side. In my TEDx talk, I talk about "reframing."[2] To *reframe* is "to frame (something) again and often in a different way."[3] It is not a complicated process, but it's not always easy to do. Basically, we take our current situation, along with all the irrational thoughts tied to it, and then we make a choice to see it differently and replace those thoughts with more rational ones. When we reframe, we tend to see the brighter side of almost any situation. If we are to survive any challenge, crisis, or adversity, reframing is the biggest tool in our arsenal.

- Learn from it. The most significant gift of adversity or challenges is the learning that can come from them. If we let those times come and go, and we have not been changed or have not learned any new behaviors, then we can absolutely call it a crisis. We build our resilience muscle when we stand in our circumstances, take a breath, and learn to be better.

- Choose a bigger mission to focus on. When speaking to others who have overcome great adversity in their lives, the one thing I consistently hear is to focus on moving forward. How can we help our people do that? We need to do as many of the leaders have expressed in this book and help those we lead find a personal mission that moves with them no matter where they go. I have found that when I focus on a mission that is bigger than myself or bigger than anything I might face, I can then put one foot in front of the other and never look back. It becomes the bull's-eye from which I never remove my focus. This is a critical tool in the arsenal of the caring leader.

Remember, we must first have adversity or challenges before we can build resilience. Leaders with heart help guide those they lead, help them have courage to face the things they are afraid to face, by sometimes modeling the process, and they pull on the collective power of the team to help too. As Frank Ricotta, founder and CEO of BurstIQ, so astutely said of leaders, "It's your job to set the course and tenor, even in uncertain times and situations.

The Art of Caring Leadership in Practice

We all face challenges and obstacles in our way; it is the leader's responsibility to help those he or she leads to meet those challenges with resolve and courage. When you feel emotion bubbling up in a situation, lean in by listening and then focus on being objective and clear-minded in your response. While you need to show empathy, your role is to help your people scale the mountain.

Caring Leader Highlight

Cynthia Grant
chief operations officer and chief clinical officer, AllHealth Network

Interviewed on: Episode 85, "Leaders with Heart Understand That Their Own Brokenness Is a Gift"

- **Industry:** Health care (community mental health)

- **Aha moment:** Cynthia attributes her career path in mental health to her turbulent childhood. "There was substance use, mental illness, domestic violence, and a lot of neglect of responsibilities by my parents, so much to the point that the Department of Human Services ultimately removed my brother and me from home," she shared. From a very young age, Cynthia had to step up and become a responsible provider and caretaker for herself and her brother. Though she knew her parents were trying their best, Cynthia recognized that they weren't capable of being the role models she needed them to be. That reality compelled her to become a better leader: "I was able to find a way to be resilient in the face of adversity, and how to channel the struggles that I have into some type of purpose. I learned that if you commit yourself to a role that has meaning and you give it your all, then things are going to be OK." As Cynthia found her calling, she carried that very strength and toughness into her professional life and realized how applicable those qualities are in a variety of roles.

- **How they embody caring leadership:** This chapter is centered on the core quality of resilience and why leaders need to develop it within themselves and pass it on to those they lead. Not only does Cynthia exemplify why resilience is key, but her professional success is a testament to the fact that resilience is often developed outside the workplace. Her past doesn't define who she is, but it has inspired her outlook on life and work: "My past is representative of my belief in my leadership—a belief in good intentions, and that people are doing the best that they can. . . . That's part of who I am, and I'm proud of that."

- **Guiding philosophy:**

  - *Failure and adversity are a natural part of the leader's journey;* it's up to you to learn from them and help others learn from them too. Cynthia says moments of failure can be valuable opportunities for growth and learning, even if you feel embarrassed by them: "There's a lot of pain and a lot of shame that comes out when we fail as leaders. And then on the flip side, the opportunity to be able to really increase your own sense of worthiness, your authenticity, and realize how you were acting outside of those values." Ultimately, an effective leader knows how to bounce back from his mistakes, grow more resilient *because of* them, and help others do the same.

10

The ROI of Caring Leadership

• • •

In a world that is increasingly driven by AI and automation, some might
believe that the value of human connection is less important. However,
leading from a perspective of caring about and supporting my team trans-
lates into increased willingness to go the extra mile and a commitment
to delivering at all costs. . . . That in turn drives greater performance.
Shawnté Cox Holland, head of culture and engagement, Vanguard

Over the years, people have implied that the "soft and fluffy" type of
leadership I talk about falls short on the ROI (return on investment) front.
Up to this point, I have referenced and highlighted the many different
leadership styles and behaviors that create more positive experiences and
deeper relationships at work.

I would be remiss if I failed to highlight some of the hard-core results that the behaviors I describe in the previous chapters create when
exhibited consistently. Businesses exist to thrive by making money, serving customers and community. I am not debating this fact. My goal is
to help with the "how." The "how" of meeting business purpose is the
thing that produces positive emotions in those who drive those business
results forward.

Caring Leadership as Strategy

Cori Burbach highlighted the following truth, which can help us to re-
shape our thinking:

I think it is so easy for all of us to get wrapped up into . . . the fire of the day at work, or I've got ten things going at work and ten things at home. So, I'm running around and . . . somebody walks into your office and wants to talk, and you say, "Gosh, I just don't have time." Right? But this is where the real work happens, whether it is . . . figuring out what an employee wants for themselves and figuring out how to coach them and help them grow, and seeing that look on their face when they get the opportunities they've been looking for. That's so important, not just for the touchy-feely heart piece, but it's also the strategic piece. Like, how do we unlock the potential in our employees so that we can meet our vision faster?

As the CEO of Service Express, a privately held company, Ron Alvesteffer did not have to disclose numbers to me as proof that his efforts toward creating a culture focused around people paid off. Nonetheless, he did share and gave us insight into the simplicity of caring leadership as a strategy:

Here's the piece that people get wrong: They think, "Do I need to focus on the numbers or focus on culture?" What they don't understand is, a great culture and focusing on the people will deliver you not only the numbers you're looking for, but they'll beat them. And they think it's one or the other. It's not binary. It's the people who deliver the results. You don't get the results without the people. And that's so hard for people to wrap their mind around because in one way, it's easier to focus on a spreadsheet and numbers and just try to push those people.

Here are the results that Ron said came directly from a change in thinking on his part and in a change in leadership behavior:

When I joined the company, we were under $3 million in revenue. Now, we're over $130 million in revenue. . . . We were at fifteen employees to now close to five hundred. So, this is not the soft stuff. The soft stuff is the hard stuff, and this is what we've used to drive these results. When people say, "Well, I need results!" I need results too, and we've gotten them, but we've gotten them through our people, with our people.

Alex Smith of the City of Memphis reported similar results when talking about how the culture changed when she shifted the organization's thinking around people. Her focus on putting "the right leaders in the right positions," ensuring that they had a strong total rewards package and much more, drove results as she described:

> When I started . . . our Glassdoor review score was 2.5, and the CEO approval rating was 32 percent, and the comments were scathing . . . about the organization and what people were experiencing. Today, if you go on Glassdoor, you'll see that our review score is 3.5 out of 5, and our CEO rating is at 91 percent. Also, from an employee engagement score perspective, when I started, our employee engagement score was at 50 percent, and now we're at the 74 percent range.

One of the most profound case studies I've seen on caring leadership is that of Garry Ridge, chairman and CEO of the WD-40 Company (see the "Caring Leader Highlight" at the end of this chapter). He is very clear about his focus on people and building a culture that employees can be proud to call home. Here are some of the hard-core results Garry shared with me:

> We've been measuring the engagement . . . for over twenty years, and we are very, very proud of the fact that our engagement is 93 percent globally, and 99 percent of our tribe members [employees] say they love to tell people they work at our company. Ninety-six percent of our tribe members say they respect their coach. Now, a coach here is like your boss. As a company, our economic engine has thrived. We've grown the market cap of the company from just over $300 million to today $2.4 billion.

We've quadrupled the revenue we have, and we've taken employee engagement from the horrible numbers that a lot of companies have to 93 percent.

It is hard to debate results like these. Cynthia Grant, of AllHealth Network, shared some impressive results, but not before she provided some background to give more context to her organization's transformation due to a people-first strategy. Cynthia divulged that her organization had had a rocky road sometime ago and had to do layoffs. Their community was also disappointed on a couple of fronts. So, they had to take time to rebuild their reputation. Then, a new CEO came in who was visionary and focused on embracing a people strategy, which was not the focus previously. Of this time, Cynthia reflected, "So, by shifting our frame and making our strategic plan the priority first to take care of our people, to make sure that they're engaged, to make sure that they have the information and the tools they need to do their job, to make sure that they have consistent supervision and support no matter what area that they work in, we went from a 30 percent and I've heard numbers as high as 42 percent turnover rate to now 19 percent in just a couple of years."

On top of this improvement, Cynthia's organization was selected, through an employee nomination process, as one of the Denver Metro area's Top Workplaces for 2019 by the *Denver Post*. Remembering this accomplishment, Cynthia said, "If you think about the return on that type of effort and focus to make sure that we're taking care of our people, not just financially but also with information and heart, and making sure that they have that voice, we have dramatically changed this organization, and I'm very proud to have been a part of that."

Loyalty as the Ultimate Gauge of ROI

While I uncovered many "proofs of concept" for embracing the caring leadership philosophy, I wanted to highlight those above and end with a truly powerful story by Andy Boian, founder and CEO of Dovetail Solutions, which directly illustrates how those led by caring leaders act in ways that produce positive business results.

When Andy first started his company, he was most concerned with how the firm would survive financially. One of his clients fell behind on paying his bills. When this happened, Andy told the team members who were assigned to this client to stop work until the client paid. One of Andy's team members stood up and offered to take that amount out of his paycheck. His team member said, "If it's about money, if we are going to slow down this process and not serve them until they pay, I don't agree. So, take it out of my paycheck . . . because they'll pay us."

Of this employee's courage and loyalty to his firm's customers, Andy thought, "Wow! I just learned something here from a colleague that I would have never picked up on because I was so squarely focused on getting bills paid." Admittedly, Andy hadn't reacted with compassion and empathy for the client. Instead, he had treated the situation like a transaction. His team member was a head of household with children, and he was willing to give up his check. Andy never did take the money from his team member. Instead, he relaxed and showed more concern for the customer. In time, that customer paid the company in full.

This is a powerful story of employee loyalty. If Andy's team member had not taken such a strong position or even felt comfortable taking a differing stance, the company would not have that loyal customer today. This example is as powerful as any I can think of for making caring leadership a top business strategy. Kimberly Loving, chief of staff for the City of Seattle's Department of Information Technology, said it perfectly: "It doesn't matter how wonderful our strategic plans may look or how excited we all are about it. If we are not seeding, developing, investing, and placing our people, our most precious and most valuable resource, at the core of everything that we do, we will fail."

When we do the things up front to show that we care for those we lead, they will do more to move us forward than we could ever imagine! As you can see from the examples above, caring leadership isn't just some nebulous concept that is hard to measure. Cori, Ron, Garry, Cynthia, Andy, and Alex all show us that this type of leadership produces positive impacts on an organization's bottom line.

Caring Leader Highlight

Garry Ridge
chairman and chief executive officer, WD-40 Company

Interviewed on: Episode 73, "Leaders with Heart Help Their People Step into the Best Versions of Themselves"

- **Industry/specialization:** Consumer goods (chemical manufacturing)

- **Aha moment:** Garry had a personal moment of reckoning when he was offered the opportunity to lead the WD-40 Company as CEO. He had to seriously think how he could best create a culture of empowered and engaged people, and how that would translate into hard business results. What did he do? "I poked around and looked for an opportunity to help me understand more of what behaviors and aspects of culture we might like to practice and to see if we can do that. I went back to school and got a master's degree in leadership," he recalled. Slowly but surely, he was forming his own impression of what needed to happen. "Organizations need to have a clear and dedicated leadership that says it's all about the people. We need to set a true purpose that people can align with. We need to have values that set people free," Garry said. He believes that if you start with a solid and compassionate culture, the business side of things will fall in place a lot easier than if everyone hated working for the company. From there, Garry developed strategies and tactics that focused equally on the emotional and economic engine of the organization and put them in action to make a difference.

- **How they embody caring leadership:** This final chapter focuses on the return on investment of caring leadership, and the success of the WD-40 Company under Garry's management indicates just how rich and robust that return can be. Garry believes "if you build amazing cultures, you build amazing organizations." He started with culture and ended with concrete results.

- **Guiding philosophy:**

  - *Caring leaders are here to help people step into the best version of their selves every day.* That simple sentence is at the core of Garry's leadership style, and perhaps at the core of this very book. When we show our employees that we authentically care for them by helping them in their personal journeys—whatever that may entail—they will go over and above for team and organizational success.

Are You Ready to Become a Caring Leader?

• • •

The measure of success is not whether you have a tough problem to deal with, but whether it's the same problem you had last year.
John Foster Dulles, former U.S. secretary of state, 1953–1959

We are at a crossroads regarding leadership. Many leaders have become increasingly deaf to the plight of those who drive their business forward. Sadly, they let their egos win the day and then expect to benefit from a workplace that is suffering from such lack of compassion and care. Many are not interested in doing the type of work, both individually and organizationally, required to set up a place where all are welcome, respected, listened to, raised up, and truly seen. This book never was for them.

I like to say that I am called to do the work that I do, with its diverse range and spaces. I don't say that because it's sexy. I say that because it's true. In every workplace where I've worked, I felt like the odd woman out or, as I have called it, "a person with five heads." This was never clearer than when I landed in a leadership role that finally put me at the executive leadership table. For as long as I can remember, I have advocated for either customers or employees. I saw myself, in many ways, as their representative at whatever table I was sitting.

While I do believe that most people want to do the right thing, and they think that they care for and even help others, I would often see more ego and one-sidedness than I hoped to see. I presented the voice of the customer (and employee) on many occasions. I sat at the leadership table to make sure they used those voices to improve things for many. Often, I

147

was met with sarcastic, defensive, privileged, and naive comments about those requests. Sometimes I would take it personally, but it was not about me. It was about the leaders at the table. They put a wall up between themselves and those who looked to them for solutions, guidance, safety, and meaningful work. They failed to express concern and kindness with any consistency.

Who we are as leaders is a culmination of our experiences. Like the artist who paints and chooses a certain color palette for each piece to elicit its own set of emotions, our leadership behaviors—the good and not-so-good stuff—are deeply personal to us. We are a mash-up, and while things happen to us on our journeys, we can make different and better choices that will determine what goes into our palette and whether or not our leadership journey turns out like a work of art.

Sometime ago, my daughter watched a documentary in school about a woman who had a salon, and all she did was help women who people might think of as "broken." These women were battered, sexually abused, or homeless. After they entered the salon, the owner fixed them up.

When they came in, these women were all jaded, hostile, and a little bit rough. Despite this fact, the salon owner loved on them and made them feel good by doing their hair and nails, massaging their cracked feet, and doing other things that the average person would not do. Within a matter of four or five hours, the women were interacting with one another. They were lifting one another up. They told each other, "You can do it!" They became sources of inspiration for one another in their pain.

The salon owner was able to break down the walls and smooth the rough edges of the women in a matter of hours. It was because she showed them concern and kindness. In her actions, she demonstrated that she cared for them.

When you are a leader, it is the love and the care that you put into your people, the focus, and the importance that you make them feel that enables them to lift up themselves. As a result, they do more for those around them. They feel better about themselves, and now they see the world differently. They are prepared to do more for their team and for you.

I remember when I came up with the name of my podcast. I was at a conference titled "No Longer Virtual," hosted by my dear friend Sarah

Elkins. Neil Hughes, a ghostwriter and the host of a very successful tech podcast, was also in attendance. When we started to talk about podcasts, Neil said he could make it easy for me—I could interview leaders and he could do all the technical things. I already knew Neil from a social media group. So, I knew I could trust him. He told me that I needed to think about a title. The very first title I thought of was "Leadership With Heart." Still, he told me to go home and think about it. After I thought about it some more, that title was still stuck in my mind.

Why? Because it is who I am, and it also represents what I dream of seeing in the world. I know that leadership with heart, or caring leadership, fills holes for those we lead, whether at home or at work. There is so much pain inside and outside of the workplace, and people are looking for leaders to make them feel cared for in genuine ways. That leader is you!

There is a complicated tension that exists for those who aspire to care more. It is complicated because we are imperfect, make mistakes, revert to our old ways often, and have glaring egos, which can make us focus on ourselves more than on others. The prerequisite to becoming a caring leader is that we are aware of the holes we are unwittingly creating for those we lead, and we have a desire to change and a willingness to do the work to fill them.

While leaders often work in teams to try to solve problems and land on decisions, leadership is an individual sport. So, when each person is more emotionally intelligent about who he is and how he impacts his world and the people in it, is more empathetic toward his people and adaptable to change, and looks to inspire those around him to greatness, then we see leadership evolution. In aggregate, then, we can decide which road to take. Leadership is a choice. Leaders have to make an infinite number of choices to either show up for those they lead or stay at home.

Ian Sohn, president and chief client officer at Hawkeye, added rich color to this when he said, "You cannot copy somebody else's version of leadership. You can . . . take bits and pieces from people you know . . . or people you admire, but at the end of the day, you have to be yourself in the way that you apply those learnings to your own leadership style. . . . There is nothing worse than somebody doing a bad imitation of another leader."

Organizations might do well one year, or one quarter, but if they are not caring for their people first, the success will not be long-lived. Organizations are made up of people. At the top of the hierarchy are a group of people who decide which buttons to press, which budgets to allot where, which people to promote, which behaviors to accept, which incentives to give. Often, it's a constant cycle of intermittent bright lights with increasingly disconnected and exclusive decision-making.

What if return on investment were not the big focus? What if organizational leaders focused first on expressing daily actions of concern and kindness for those they led? What if this new focus put much more effort on developing leaders and gauging their effectiveness by asking employees and customers their opinion? Can you see how this new focus would produce the currency of loyalty, productivity, and innovation?

Imagine work that is not a drag but uplifting, and when heading into work, employees say, "I know I am cared for and I can't wait to make my manager, team, and organization look good!" instead of "I wish I didn't have to go to work with these people who don't care for me or even know me." That would be a great day, wouldn't it? We can get there.

Where Do We Go from Here?

Here is the thing: it starts with you. Yeah! Don't turn around—I am talking to you! You can change how you make those you lead feel. You can make a choice to change your mindset and behaviors to be more in line with the principles in this book. You can go against the grain of leaders who say that they care but never genuinely express that care to those who hope for that treatment.

How can you show that you care, specifically?

- Lead yourself first.

- Make your people feel important.

- Look for the greatness in those you lead.

- Involve those you lead in the solution.

- Meet your people where they are.

- Empower those you lead to make their own decisions.

- Provide your people safe spaces in which to share countering or creative opinions.

- Listen to those your lead.

- Help them to become more resilient in changing times.

I love the quote from John Foster Dulles at the top of this chapter because it perfectly highlights why increasing our accountability to express caring leadership matters. I wrote this book because I hoped to uplift teams and organizations everywhere. I cannot live up to that desire if I do not, in some way, provide a way for leaders to measure their level of caring leadership, work to improve how they express that care through daily actions, and have a source of support and guidance. In short, I will have failed in my mission if leadership behaviors go unchanged.

As I have stated throughout this book, every manager thinks he or she is and wants to be a caring leader, but most of us fall short in various ways. Although I have outlined the behaviors that leaders need to demonstrate in order to translate the desire to be a caring leader into a reality, I feel compelled to help you remain accountable in demonstrating the daily actions that show concern and kindness toward those you lead.

How to Remain Accountable

Before I go into detail about my accountability system, let me share something interesting about myself. I am more of a visionary leader who relates with others and builds rapport quickly. I take great pride in growing others, work hard to communicate with others in the way they need to hear it, and empathize with those who might be considered underdogs. Having said that, one thing I am not is someone who loves to sit in data and spreadsheets. I dislike details. That is ironic, given that I am a nonpracticing attorney.

Because I have always felt called to advocate for those who don't have a voice or are not invited to the decision-making table, I actually enjoy diving deep into the data of employee engagement or culture surveys, or sitting and listening intently to employees in focus groups and culture teams. Why is that different from any other data? It is because my "why" requires that I do it, and my "why" is stronger than the pain of sitting in the details.

I want to get to the truth! I need to get to the truth and communicate that truth to the executive leaders who can do something about what they learn. My doing this helps to change leaders' minds and their behaviors. This change improves employee experience, which increases engagement and retention. Therefore, data, accountability, and follow-through are critical to the long-term expression of caring leadership.

As I embarked on writing this book, I intuitively knew that you would want a way to measure how much of a caring leader you are and a way forward to grow in the behaviors in the book. To that extent, I worked with a renowned industrial and organizational psychology firm to create a robust self-assessment that will serve as the first step of measurement and accountability.

A Closer Look at the Assessment Process

Many self-assessments are more self-serving than useful. Those that are useful often lack the depth of recommendations or a support and guidance system to help us remain accountable to the changes we want. I spent considerable time framing out the questions to align with the nine main behaviors and sub-behaviors in the book. Then I created an algorithm that will provide areas of focus based upon your responses.

Along with the assessment, you will have access to the Caring Leadership online community, which will be moderated by me and members of my team. There, you will find a learning academy of courses with suggestions customized to your areas of focus, based upon your assessment results and recommendations. The greater community will act as a support and guidance system to help you decipher the finer points of your leadership journey.

You will also have access to mastermind groups, where I and my team will facilitate discussions and help crystallize action plans. Moreover, I will create other assessment tools that help the measurement and assessment process as the community provides feedback about what they need and expect from the community.

Additionally, inside the community I will highlight several coaches who will be available to work through your assessment results with you and help you stay on the right path to caring leadership.

Why Enlist Help to Assess and Change?

One might argue that it would be difficult for any one individual to accurately assess how "caring" he or she is as a leader. While I have attempted to make the assessment process one that will enlighten even the most naive and provide valuable next steps to change, the results will be even more insightful if reviewed by both the assessment taker and a coach or mentor.

I am an executive leadership coach. Personally, I find it very helpful when my client has completed some sort of development assessment that we can use as a launchpad for our coaching sessions. It allows me to review and parse through the finer points ahead of time and then again when sitting with the leader who hopes to get better. Moreover, it helps both of us pinpoint exactly where we need to focus.

Without my third-party view of the assessment results and my guidance for next steps, my clients have reported that they often flounder. This is not me selling me. This is me expressing concern and kindness toward you and suggesting a richer course of action for more fruitful results. The road to becoming more of a caring leader can be a long and hard one with lots of ups and downs. Don't try to do it alone.

Lastly, the Caring Leadership online community will further serve to clarify any questions that "caring leaders in development" might have. This community will also provide the mutual feedback and support that is often lacking in leadership.

So, there you have it! You are almost at the end of this book, but you get to decide where you are in your caring leadership journey. You can choose to finish this book and be done with all of this concern and kindness talk. My hope? That you stay with me on this journey, and you take the Caring Leadership Self-Assessment (the invitation and link follow this chapter) and dive right into the accountability structure I created for you.

Know that you are not in this alone. Leaders from around the globe are entering this journey with you. Caring leadership is more art than science, because only you can determine the different hues of your behaviors. Caring leadership is taking daily actions in ways that show concern and kindness to those we lead.

Only you can determine how you treat those you lead. Only you can transform your desire to care with the true expression of care. The exciting news is that you have the brush, you have the palette, and you can determine what your canvas will become.

No matter where you start, no matter where you live, no matter your industry, you have the power to change how you show up. You can care more and uplift your team and your organization. I promise you this journey will not be in vain. Lives will change! You will see positive results! If each leader commits to this type of change, we will awaken the sleeping giants in our global workforces to be more and achieve more and create a healthier society. We can create a beautiful canvas of connected, loving cultures filled with people who truly care for one another and produce beautiful art, together!

As the famous philosopher Socrates once said, "The secret of change is to focus all of your energy, not on fighting the old, but on building the new." I have provided some tools for you to use to create something new and wonderful so that you may produce a legacy of care that will endure!

THE CARING LEADERSHIP
SELF-ASSESSMENT

Hopefully *The Art of Caring Leadership* has proven the radical power and importance of caring support in the workplace and provided you with the necessary strategies to make employees feel included and valued. Now that you see why caring for your employees is in fact an imperative for your own and others' success, I invite you to take the first step toward unlocking your full leadership potential by completing **The Caring Leadership Self-Assessment.**

The Caring Leadership Self-Assessment will help you identify the level of care you are extending to your employees and what steps you can take to become a more empathetic and heart-centered leader. Whether you're seeking customer satisfaction, increased productivity, or employee engagement, improving the success of your team and your organization starts with you.

TAKE THE ASSESSMENT ONLINE AT THECARINGLEADERSHIPSELFASSESSMENT.COM, AND BEGIN YOUR LEADERSHIP JOURNEY TODAY

Guest Appendix

• • •

Throughout this book, I've drawn from a rich archive of almost one hundred interviews I've conducted with diverse leaders on my podcast, *Leadership With Heart*. The podcast highlights the strengths of caring leaders, their trials and victories, and practical advice on how to become more emotionally intelligent leaders. Here you will find more information on these guests and the *Leadership With Heart* episode they were featured on.

Kirk Adams, PhD, is the president and chief executive officer of the American Foundation for the Blind (AFB), a national nonprofit of forty-one employees that expands possibilities for people with vision loss. In his role, Kirk pursues strategic relationships with peers, policy makers, and employers to accelerate systemic advancement. He was interviewed on Episode 109, "Leaders with Heart Often Find Their 'Why' Through Their Adversity."

Ray Aguirre is the chief of police at California State University, Fullerton. The CSUF Police Department is committed to providing quality service to a leading campus of the CSU network and facilitating its academic mission. As the chief of police, Ray is cognizant of the important role that public safety plays on a university campus and recognizes that educational law enforcement's task is to develop healthy relationships with the community. He was interviewed on Episode 27, "Leaders with Heart Lead with Purpose."

Jandel Allen-Davis, MD, is the president and chief executive officer of Craig Hospital, a world-renowned private, not-for-profit rehabilitation hospital and research center that specializes in the care of people who have sustained a spinal cord or brain injury. In this capacity, Jandel oversees more than one thousand employees at Craig Hospital. She was interviewed on Episode 66, "Leaders with Heart Show Up and Speak Up."

Ron Alvesteffer is the president and chief executive officer of Service Express, a privately traded company with more than five hundred employees that specializes in on-site data center hardware maintenance services. During his tenure at Service Express, Ron has helped Service Express define its market and create a unique performance-driven culture. He was interviewed on Episode 92, "Leaders with Heart Know That Spending Time with Their People Drives Business Results."

Rhoda Banks is the vice president, head of talent management, at Rabo Agri-Finance, a privately held financial services provider for leading agricultural producers. In her current role, Rhoda serves as a thought partner for business leaders, understanding the business needs and strategic goals of designing and leveraging a global talent management strategy to develop high-quality talent. She was interviewed on Episode 80, "Leaders with Heart Understand They Are the Caretakers of Their Employees' Futures."

Howard Behar previously served as president of the Starbucks Coffee Company, a publicly traded American multinational chain of coffeehouses and roastery reserves with more than 250,000 employees. During his tenure, he participated in the growth of the company from only twenty-eight stores to more than fifteen thousand stores spanning five continents. He served on the Starbucks Board of Directors for twelve years before retiring. Howard was interviewed on Episode 82, "Leaders with Heart Live True Servant Leadership."

Sarah Bernhardt is the vice president of people at Greystone Technology, a privately held company with seventy-five-plus team members providing information technology services, including IT consulting and implementation, digital marketing, and web design/development services. Among her various responsibilities, Sarah leads and mentors the People and Training teams, and she drives culture through hiring, onboarding, organizational development, and strategic performance management. She was interviewed on Episode 52, "Leaders with Heart Use Empathy to Understand Their People."

Megan Bertrand is the senior vice president of learning and development at FirstBank, Colorado's second-largest depository institution and Colorado's largest locally owned/privately held bank, with a commitment to convenience and loyalty to its three thousand employees. As SVP of learning and development, Megan is responsible for driving leadership programs and remodeling the company's training center. She was interviewed on Episode 61, "Leaders with Heart Form Friendships with Their People."

Sarah Bierenbaum is the founder and principal of Sarah B Consulting, a consultancy and sole proprietorship that empowers start-ups and scale-ups with the specific tools, relationships, and processes necessary to flourish and optimize their teams. As an executive leader, mentor, and entrepreneur, Sarah motivates teams to build scalable solutions, tackle complex problems, and embrace change in the rapid-growth software as a service (SaaS) environment. She previously led a team of twenty as a senior director of the Customer Success team at Olo. Sarah was interviewed on Episode 7, "Why Leaders with Heart Provide Safe Spaces for Their People."

Andy Boian is the founder and chief executive officer of Dovetail Solutions, a public relations, branding, and positioning firm based in Denver that provides business-to-business services. As CEO of a privately held, top full-service PR firm, Andy works with clients to build mutually beneficial relationships to maximize opportunities. He was interviewed on Episode 112, "Leaders with Heart Lead First with Grace."

Andy Books is the sales manager at Salelytics, a privately traded outsourcing/offshoring company and one of the nation's leading providers of inside sales, account management, and inbound support services. As sales manager, Andy leads a team of seventeen sales associates who connect with customers to seek out incremental growth opportunities for a premier air and freight express/ground transportation company. He was interviewed on Episode 2, "Leaders with Heart Have Integrity as Their North Star."

Patrick Brady is a regional president at FirstBank, Colorado's second-largest depository institution and Colorado's largest locally owned/privately held bank, with a commitment to convenience and loyalty to its three thousand employees. In this capacity, Patrick oversees and guides seven bank markets in three states with thirty-four branches and over $4 billion in assets. His teams concentrate on customer development, balance-sheet growth, industry-leading profitability, community engagement, and strategic vision. He was interviewed on Episode 47, "Leaders with Heart Go Personal with Their People."

Steve Browne is the vice president of human resources at LaRosa's Pizzeria, Inc., the leading pizzeria and Italian restaurant in the greater Cincinnati area, with thirteen locations and more than 1,100 team members. Steve provides strategic leadership for all facets of human resources for various team members throughout several company locations. He was interviewed on Episode 71, "Leaders with Heart Understand What Drives Their People."

Cori Burbach is the assistant city manager for the City of Dubuque in Iowa. She assists the city manager in directing the day-to-day operations of the city government and plays a key role in creating a more data-driven, high-performance organization focusing on outcomes, including cross-departmental cooperation across the 700 city employees. She was interviewed on Episode 96, "Leaders with Heart Understand That Leadership Is about Courage and Vulnerability."

Phil Burgess is the chief people and operations officer at C Space, a public global customer agency with more than 450 employees that works with brands to build customers into the ways that companies work and deliver on "Customer Inspired Growth." In this role, Phil drives strategic cultural and operational initiatives that support the growth of C Space's people, business, and clients. He was interviewed on Episode 81, "Leaders with Heart Embrace the Mess of Humanness in the Workplace."

Jennifer Butler is the executive vice president and general manager at Innate Pharma, Inc., a public biotech company with more than two hundred employees, dedicated to improving treatment for patients through therapeutic antibodies that harness the immune system to fight cancer. Jennifer has more than twenty years of pharmaceutical and biotechnology experience across several therapeutic areas and functions, including global marketing and analytics, and corporate strategy. She was interviewed on Episode 6, "Why Leaders with Heart Know That They Cannot Do It Alone."

Chris Chancey is the founder and chief executive officer of Amplio Recruiting, a public staffing agency that helps bridge the hiring needs of US companies and the career needs of reliable talent within the refugee workforce in the country. Chris is focused on achieving Amplio's vision of staffing companies in twenty-five locations by 2025 and providing operational and financial support to the entire Amplio team. He was interviewed on Episode 75, "Leaders with Heart Work to Create Shared Trust."

Phil Cohen is the founder and president of Cohen Architectural Woodworking, an award-winning, family-owned commercial woodworking firm headquartered in St. James, Missouri. Utilizing a direct-to-vendor model, Phil works with owners, construction managers, interior designers, and architects in some of the country's largest companies to meet their specific functional requirements. He was interviewed on Episode 69, "Leaders with Heart Invest in the Potential of Their People."

Shawnté Cox Holland is the head of culture and engagement at Vanguard, one of the world's largest investment companies, supported by more than seventeen thousand employees, offering a large selection of high-quality, low-cost mutual funds; ETFs; advice; and related services. Shawnté applies innovative and research-based approaches to practices such as organizational design, team management, and leadership development to create high-value outputs for organizations. She was interviewed on Episode 84, "Leaders with Heart Understand That Leadership Is to Be Learned, Studied and Explored."

Don Davis is the county manager of Jefferson County in Colorado, which has a population of more than 580,000 people. After retiring from the military, Don joined Jeffco in 2017 as county manager; at Jeffco he enjoys serving alongside more than three thousand dedicated employees. He was interviewed on Episode 97, "Leaders with Heart Have a Clear Leadership Vision."

Tom Dietzler is the director of operations at St. Peter Lutheran Church and School, a 152-year-old church and school in Appleton, Wisconsin, with more than two thousand members, two campuses, about fifty employees, and a budget of $2.5 million. Tom is responsible for managing the building and campus, recruiting volunteers, and overseeing a team of twelve. He was interviewed on Episode 9, "Leaders with Heart Know That They Must Connect With Their People Consistently to Be Trusted."

Melissa Eovine is the manager of sponsorships for the Fellowship of Catholic University Students (FOCUS), a Catholic outreach sharing the hope and joy of the gospel with university students. Melissa works with sponsoring organizations at FOCUS events to identify and execute win-win outcomes. She was interviewed on Episode 57, "Leaders with Heart Create Psychological Safety for Their Teams."

Jennifer Fairweather is the director of human resources for Jefferson County in Colorado, where she works with more than three thousand other County employees. In this role, Jennifer partners with County leaders in matters relating to employee relations and organizational development, facilitates culture change initiatives toward increased accountability and employee engagement, and reorganizes functions to enhance customer service. She was interviewed on Episode 95, "Leaders with Heart Care for the Whole Person That They Lead."

Mindy Flanigan is the founder and chief inspiration officer at Inspiring HR, a private human resources consultancy that provides employee management services to small businesses, typically those with fewer than fifty employees. Mindy's background includes compliance, employee management best practices, and payroll and benefits. Mindy's time spent in human resources services has given her a unique understanding of how to make HR simple and valuable for small businesses. She was interviewed on Episode 38, "Leaders with Heart Don't Shy Away from Admitting Their Love for Their People."

Kristy McCann Flynn is cofounder and CEO of GoCoach, a professional coaching organization that delivers coaching at scale. Kristy is a strategic human resources leader with a focus on change management and organizational development. She was interviewed on Episode 50, "Leaders with Heart Know That Their Lens Impacts Those They Lead."

Keith Freier is the director of operational systems and technology at Pacific Northwest National Laboratory (PNNL), a national lab with more than 4,500 employees, taking on some of the world's greatest science and technology challenges. In his current position, Keith specializes in operationalizing science through the integration of technology, policy, and field operations to deliver mission-critical solutions. He was interviewed on Episode 25, "Leaders with Heart Understand That Attitude Reflects Leadership."

Dirk Frese is the vice president of sales, marketing, and service at Julabo USA, a private manufacturing company specializing in temperature control products used in laboratories, research centers, and industry. Julabo USA employs fifty people, and its mother company in Germany employs more than four hundred. Dirk specializes in chemistry, biochemistry, biotechnology, and microbiology, with a subspecialty in global sales and marketing. He was interviewed on Episode 19, "Leaders with Heart Take a Holistic Approach in Building Relationships with Their Employees."

Cheryl Fullerton is the executive vice president, people and communications, at Corus Entertainment, a publicly traded media and content company based in Canada, developing and delivering high-quality content across platforms for audiences around the world. As an EVP, Cheryl is accountable for the people, culture, and corporate communications elements of Corus's business strategy. This includes leading the creation of a high-performance culture to support the company's 3,500+ people. She was interviewed on Episode 98, "Leaders with Heart Create Psychological Safety for All."

Rich Gassen is the printing production manager at the University of Wisconsin–Madison (UW–Madison), a public institution serving more than forty thousand students, offering a complete spectrum of liberal arts studies and student activities. Rich oversees operations of preflight, plating, process color, and spot color offset printing, bindery, and deliveries at UW–Madison's full-service printing facility, and leads others to be empowered and make decisions on their own. He was interviewed on Episode 32, "Leaders with Heart Know That They Must Show Up and Participate."

Cynthia Grant is the chief operations officer and chief clinical officer of All-Health Network, a nonprofit health care organization providing a full spectrum of behavioral health care to more than seventeen thousand children, adults, families, and couples in ten unique settings. As a member of the executive team, Cynthia participates in contract negotiations, budgeting, grant writing, marketing, and strategic planning. She was interviewed on Episode 85, "Leaders with Heart Understand That Their Own Brokenness Is a Gift."

Brigitte Grimm is the chief deputy treasurer of Larimer County in north central Colorado, which has a population of more than 350,000 people. Prior to this role, Brigitte served for eight years as treasurer for Adams County, where she was responsible for collecting all county property taxes, distributing those taxes to the underlying taxing authorities, and investing the difference on behalf of the county. She was interviewed on Episode 3, "Leaders with Heart Clear the Path So Their People Can Do Great Work."

Heather Heebner is the vice president of human resources at Instant Financial, an earned wage access and pay card solution that gives employees free access to pay after every shift. With more than twenty-two years of hands-on experience, Heather enjoys coaching all levels of leadership relating to employee engagement, best practices, and change management. Most recently, she has served as the HR leader for several mergers and acquisitions. She was interviewed on Episode 24, "Leaders with Heart Strive to Serve First."

Tim Hinchey III is the president and chief executive officer of USA Swimming, the national governing body for swimming in the United States, serving more than four hundred thousand members and creating opportunities for swimmers and coaches of all backgrounds to participate. Tim has held leadership positions in the United States and United Kingdom for organizations such as Major League Soccer, the English Premier League, the National Basketball Association, and the National Hockey League. He was interviewed on Episode 16, "Leaders with Heart Know That They Have an Obligation to Grow the People They Lead."

Nate Igielinski is the service and parts field operations manager at FCA Fiat and Chrysler Automobiles, responsible for the after-sales (retail/wholesale of MOPAR parts and customer retention growth) involving eighteen area managers; eleven states; and 309 Chrysler, Dodge, Jeep, Ram, and Fiat FCA franchised dealerships. He was interviewed on Episode 11, "Leaders with Heart Work Hard Not to Harden Their Hearts."

Eric Jacobsen is the chief operating officer at Kalnin Ventures, a private values-driven firm seeking to invest in attractive upstream oil and gas opportunities, composed of a small team of almost thirty employees. Eric has a long history of successful project development and operations delivery spanning more than twenty-three years and across the oil and gas industry. He was interviewed on Episode 23, "Leaders with Heart Understand That in Order to Catch Fish You Must Cast among Them."

Udaiyan (U.J.) Jatar is the founder and CEO of Blue Earth Network, a private management consulting firm and a fully integrated innovation hub created with a 100 percent focus on transformational growth/impact. U.J. and his team train and support leaders of start-up, midsize, and global organizations to discover, invent, brand, and scale transformative businesses. He was interviewed on Episode 39, "Leaders with Heart Look for Greatness Inside the People They Lead."

Carey Jenkins is the chief executive officer at Substantial, a private digital product studio that offers clients best-in-class software that lowers risk and creates faster outcomes through strategy, design, and development for web, mobile, and connected devices. As CEO of Substantial, Carey encourages more women to seize leadership opportunities and impact overall workforce growth. She also brings expertise in client relationship management, delivery management, and business development. She was interviewed on Episode 62, "Leaders with Heart Understand That Leadership Is an Iterative Process."

Christinne Johnson is the president of human resources at FirstBank, Colorado's second-largest depository institution and largest locally owned/privately held bank, with a commitment to convenience and loyalty to its three thousand employees. Christinne oversees talent recruitment, benefits, compensation and payroll administration, retirement plan administration, and compliance with employment and labor laws. She was interviewed on Episode 21, "Leaders with Heart Give Themselves the Grace of Imperfection."

Karen Johnson is an equity and inclusion administrator at the Washington Department of Corrections, the second-largest state agency in Washington, employing more than 8,600 staff members who work throughout the state in twelve prison facilities, sixteen work releases, multiple field offices, and several headquarters offices. Karen serves as the department's expert and adviser on equity, diversity, and inclusion, and is responsible for increasing awareness of those values. She was interviewed on Episode 106, "Leaders with Heart Are Human and Give Others Permission to Be the Same."

Jill Katz is the founder and chief change officer at Assemble HR Consulting, a private boutique human resources firm that focuses on culture, communication, and conflict. Jill works closely alongside the six other Assemble HR Consulting employees to help executives see the value in relationships and how focusing on authentic communication can result in better business results. She is best known for her "3C's Approach": candor, courage, and care. She was interviewed on Episode 59, "Leaders with Heart Understand That Leadership Equals Relationship."

Joe Kwon is the associate director of the Global Privacy and Information Management Office at KPMG US, one of the world's leading professional financial services firms, with ninety offices and more than twenty-nine thousand employees. As associate director, Joe facilitates the cross-border transfer of information through creation of standardized privacy policies, responds to client inquiries, and maintains the KPMG internal privacy framework. He was interviewed on Episode 34, "Leaders with Heart Understand That They Must Truly Connect with Their People First to Build Trust."

John LaFemina is the executive director of performance management and the chief risk officer for the Pacific Northwest National Laboratory (PNNL), a national lab with more than 4,500 employees and a global reach. John is responsible for a broad scope of enterprise-level activities, including contract oversight, executing key institutional risk management functions, and guiding the development of a comprehensive set of performance management metrics. He was interviewed on Episode 41, "Leaders with Heart Are Genuine, Allowing Those Who They Lead to Be the Same."

Kimberly Loving is the chief of staff for the City of Seattle's Department of Information Technology. Kimberly is responsible for overseeing thirteen thousand employees and for the strategic and operational leadership of department-wide functional areas including human resources, workforce equity, diversity and inclusion, and organizational change management. She was interviewed on Episode 104, "Leaders with Heart Cultivate and Invest in Their People."

LaToya Lyn is vice president of talent strategy at Oscar Health, a health insurance company. LaToya leads strategic HR across the entire business through a growth stage with more than sixteen hundred employees. She leads a team of more than thirty HR professionals across diversity, inclusion, and belonging; HR directors and business partners; employee relations and learning and development. She was interviewed on Episode 130, "Leaders with Heart Create a Space for Others to Follow."

Ethan Mann is the chief executive officer at Validus Cellular Therapeutics, Inc., a preclinical pharmaceutical company in Aurora, Colorado, developing a novel stem cell–based approach to augment antibiotic efficacy and combat resistant infections. Ethan also serves on National Institutes of Health review panels to evaluate small business innovation research grants that support the creation of small businesses nationally. He was interviewed on Episode 78, "Leaders with Heart Intentionally Drive a Sense of Purpose in Those They Lead."

Scott McCarthy is an army logistics officer with the Canadian Forces and a chief leadership officer at Moving Forward Leadership, a coaching consultancy. As an army logistics officer, Scott specializes in movement and transportation operations to support the hundred-thousand-plus members. As a chief leadership officer, Scott conducts weekly podcast interviews with guests on all facets of leadership and organization theory and helps clients sharpen various skills to help them lead their organizations. He was interviewed on Episode 12, "Leaders with Heart Build a Team Before They Need One."

Daniel McCollum is the founder and chief executive officer at Torrent Consulting, a Platinum Salesforce Partner helping businesses grow through sales, service, and marketing automation solutions. As CEO, Daniel uses his fifteen-plus years of project management and technology solution experience across various technologies to successfully oversee more than a hundred employees and five locations across two countries. He was interviewed on Episode 49, "Leaders with Heart Speak the Future into the People They Lead."

Adam McCoy is the director of human resources at Arrow Electronics, a global provider of electronic products, services, and solutions, with a network of more than 336 locations and 19,300 employees worldwide. In this role, Adam designs HR solutions for multiple global and corporate functions, and facilitates the creation and implementation of succession pipelines to meet critical business priorities. He is also the president of the Mile High Society of Human Resources Management. He was interviewed on Episode 48, "Leaders with Heart Are Fiercely Loyal to Their People."

Mareo McCracken is the chief customer officer of Movemedical, a privately held online platform composed of forty employees that simplifies and unifies the surgery case management process. Mareo's focus is to unite the marketing, sales, and success teams around the customer, creating a cohesive experience. He also guides the various customer success, business strategy, and revenue operations. He was interviewed on Episode 35, "Leaders with Heart Know

That Their Leadership Is Formed by the Conversations They Have with Their People."

Steve McIntosh is the founder and CEO of CML Offshore Recruitment, a niche recruitment and immigration services firm out of the Cayman Islands. Steve has strategic management and operational oversight including HR, IT, and marketing. He was interviewed on Episode 63, "Leaders with Heart Know That They Need Followers Before They Can Lead."

Peter Melby is the CEO of Greystone Technology, which is a firm that provides technology services including comprehensive IT management, IT service augmentation, web application development, digital marketing, and strategic consulting. Based in Denver and Fort Collins, Colorado, his firm has seventy-five employees. He was interviewed on Episode 56, "Leaders with Heart Ask the Right Questions to Understand the People They Lead."

Arlene Mendoza is the senior innovation program manager at Alluma, an organization that works collaboratively with clients and partners to unlock the possibilities of both technology and policy, helping them strengthen their communities and public support systems. She was interviewed on Episode 110, "Leaders with Heart Listen and Then Iterate."

Mark Nagel is the senior manager at Southwest Airlines—HR Transformation/ Employee Services. Mark oversees the People Services Support team and takes a lead role on many key projects within HR. He was interviewed in Episode 15, "Leaders with Heart Make Their People Feel Safe by Allowing Their Voices to Be Heard."

David Niu is the founder and CEO of TINYhr, an organization that creates software that allows organizational leaders to listen to, engage, and retain their employees. David is also the author of *Careercation: Trading Briefcase for Suitcase to Find Entrepreneurial Happiness*. He was interviewed on Episode 40, "Leaders with Heart Know That Providing Growth for the Team Is No Tiny Matter."

P. Joseph O'Neill is the chief executive officer at G&D Integrated, which is a privately owned company located in Central Illinois that focuses on logistics services. Joe joined G&D Integrated in 1989, and he is responsible for managing the overall operations and resources of the company. Prior to joining

G&D, Joe practiced bankruptcy law in the Twin Cities in Minnesota. He has led and managed the organization through economic expansion and contraction through the years. More recently, Joe's focus has been on expanding the geographic reach of the company and the diversification of G&D's customer base. Joe was interviewed on Episode 89, "Leaders with Heart Make It Safe to Speak the Truth."

Kevin Patterson is the chief executive officer of Connect for Health Colorado, the dominant health insurance marketplace of Colorado, offering individuals, families, and small employers a new online platform for exclusive access to financial assistance. As a results-oriented leader, Kevin monitors employee development and systems improvement, and helps administrative structures improve performance by focusing on core business goals and intentional thinking. He was interviewed on Episode 113, "Leaders with Heart Set a Clear Vision for Others to Follow."

Steve Paul is a principal consultant at Six68 Consulting Group and the former president of SPCS, Inc., a general contractor serving HOAs, property managers, community managers, attorneys, engineers, and architects. Six68 is committed to finding long-term solutions for their clients. Steve has extensive success as a revenue grower and team builder, and is an avid customer-facing networker who thrives on facilitating partnerships and closing deals. He was interviewed on Episode 4, "Leaders with Heart Make People Feel Important."

Robert Pepper is the senior vice president of marketing at Excel Medical, which was recently acquired by Hillrom, a public global medical device provider of more than ten thousand employees with a mission to enhance outcomes for patients and caregivers around the world. Robert is a visionary sales, marketing, and financial strategist as well as motivational leader who builds strong internal teams and partnerships to consistently deliver exceptional results. He was interviewed on Episode 10, "Leaders with Heart See the Potential in Their People and Allow Them to Flourish."

Mike Pritchard is the chief financial officer at Volunteers of America Colorado, a nonprofit, faith-based organization dedicated to helping those in need transform their lives. Mike leads the finance, human resources, and information technology functions, and directs various strategic architecture policy planning initiatives. He was interviewed on Episode 36, "Leaders with Heart Make Accountability a Priority."

Farouk Rajab is a general manager at Marriott International, Inc., a multinational hospitality company encompassing more than 7,300 properties in 134 countries and more than 170,000 employees. Farouk leads and manages a 351-room landmark hotel in downtown Providence, Rhode Island, and is responsible for planning, directing, and improving hospitality operations against aggressive requirements. He was interviewed on Episode 37, "Leaders with Heart Are Great Followers First."

Jim Reuter is the president and chief executive officer at FirstBank, Colorado's second-largest depository institution and Colorado's largest locally owned/privately held bank, with a commitment to convenience and loyalty to its three thousand employees. Jim previously served as chief operating officer of FirstBank, where he oversaw many of the bank's divisions, including loan/mortgage operations, contact center, and treasury management. FirstBank has attributed many of the bank's innovations to Jim's leadership. He was interviewed on Episode 17, "Leaders with Heart Discern When Total Transparency Is Warranted and Then Exhibit It."

Frank Ricotta is the founder and chief executive officer of BurstIQ, the leading provider of blockchain-enabled data network solutions for the health care industry. The company's private data network allows health systems and pharma and life science companies to unlock the full potential of health-related data. As CEO, Frank utilizes a versatile skill set that includes organization development, information security, product and technology strategy, and enterprise content management. He was interviewed on Episode 114, "Leaders with Heart Strike a Balance between Heart and Drive."

Garry Ridge is the chairman of the board and chief executive officer of the WD-40 Company, a publicly traded, global sales and marketing company delivering easy-to-use solutions for a wide variety of maintenance needs. Garry's responsibilities include senior management, strategic planning, managing $350 million in revenue growth and corporate culture development, directing marketing efforts in more than 160 countries, and directly overseeing 350 employees. He was interviewed on Episode 73, "Leaders with Heart Help Their People Step into the Best Versions of Themselves."

Jo-Ann Robertson is partner and chief executive officer at Ketchum London, a global communications consultancy of more than two thousand employees creating impact through a human-centered approach. Jo-Ann engages and attracts the best talent and winning clients, and manages the commercial/financial health of the company. In addition, Jo-Ann serves as the chair of the Young Women's Trust, a charity working to achieve economic justice for young women. She was interviewed on Episode 91, "Leaders with Heart Are Open to All Feedback."

T. Renata Robinson, PhD, is the chief human resources officer at the Colorado Coalition for the Homeless, a nonprofit pursuing the prevention of homelessness throughout Colorado. Renata is committed to cultivating an inclusive culture, bolstering employee morale, developing leadership skills, and implementing inclusive human resource initiatives. She is also the principal and chief people officer of her consulting practice Meek Advantages, LLC. Renata was interviewed on Episode 105, "Leaders with Heart Understand That If Their People Fail, They Fail."

Chuck Runyon is the cofounder and chief executive officer of Self Esteem Brands, the parent company of Anytime Fitness, Basecamp Fitness, and Provision Security Solutions, among others. Chuck's mission is to enrich the lives of all his clients and customers in nearly thirty countries on five continents worldwide, across three thousand independent franchises operated by 550 employees. Chuck was interviewed on Episode 77, "Leaders with Heart Understand That There Is an Emotional Investment to Being a Leader."

Patty Salazar is the executive director of the Colorado Department of Regulatory Agencies (DORA), a government administration of nearly six hundred employees, dedicated to preserving the integrity of the marketplace. Patty oversees the Colorado Office of Policy, Research, and Regulatory Reform, which ensures sensible regulation, as well as the Office of Broadband Deployment, which helps expand statewide broadband access. Patty was interviewed on Episode 28, "Leaders with Heart Know That It Takes a Village to Lead Well."

Benilda Samuels is the vice president of programs at the Rose Community Foundation, a nonprofit advancing inclusive Greater Denver communities through values-driven philanthropy. Benilda directs the programs' staff in granting approximately $10 million annually. She previously served as the chief operating officer for Nurse-Family Partnership, where she managed a $15 million budget and led teams in developing strategic plans and scaling their programs. Benilda was interviewed on Episode 103, "Leaders with Heart Help Others to Take a Breath through Adversity."

Judith Scimone is senior vice president and chief talent officer at MetLife, a public and global provider of life insurance, annuities, employee benefits, and asset management. Judith applies her years of experience in talent management, which include acting as the director of talent management at Google and holding various HR, diversity and inclusion, and consulting roles at Johnson & Johnson, Motorola, Bank of America, and Hewitt Associates. She was interviewed on Episode 45, "Leaders with Heart Leave a Legacy of People and Impact."

Trent Selbrede is a general manager at Marriott International, Inc., a multinational hospitality company encompassing more than 7,300 properties in 134 countries and 170,000+ employees. Trent manages a 288-room residence in California, which includes implementing incremental revenue strategies to earn an additional $300,000 in top-line revenue and resolving staffing shortages through retention strategies and culture building. He was interviewed on Episode 13, "Leaders with Heart Know Themselves First."

Scott Shay is the cofounder and chairman of Signature Bank, a publicly owned, full-service commercial bank of more than a thousand employees serving the financial needs of privately owned businesses and their senior managers who often find themselves underserved by the area's larger financial institutions. Scott is also the chairman of the Investment Committee of the Elah Fund, an Israeli private equity fund, and a passionate community activist, having started an adult educational program and chaired several major Jewish educational programs. Scott was interviewed on Episode 117, "Leaders with Heart Live by the Golden Rule."

Claude Silver is the chief heart officer of VaynerMedia, a social-first digital shop that focuses on storytelling across platforms and building creative campaigns. VaynerMedia is a privately held company with almost eight hundred employees. Claude's mission is to discover new ways to create spaces in which people can thrive, and bring growth opportunities to them with professional growth workshops. She was interviewed on Episode 55, "Leaders with Heart Hold Space to Truly Connect with Their People."

Sheryl Simmons is the CEO of 3flightsHR, a human resources consultancy that bridges the gap between people strategy and business strategy. Sheryl is a passionate business leader with extensive human resources, compliance, and legal experience, and serves as an executive thought leader with expertise in culture development. She previously served as the chief human resources officer at Maestro Health. Sheryl was interviewed on Episode 76, "Leaders with Heart Seek to Fill Emotional Bank Accounts."

Aaron Skogen is the general manager at Aquatix by Landscape Structures, Inc., a recreational facilities and mechanical services production company that offers a full line of water park equipment. Aaron is responsible for providing overall leadership and direction to the Aquatix team and supporting a highly engaged and dedicated culture. He also directs various activities of Aquatix including sales, marketing, engineering, project management, logistics, and installations. Aaron was interviewed as part of the Enlightened Leader Series on the *Leadership With Heart* podcast.

Nick Smarrelli is the chief executive officer at GadellNet Consulting Services, a St. Louis- and Indianapolis-based IT consulting group that helps small and medium business and education clients find solutions and secure opportunities for growth. Nick drives operational efficiencies, enhances GadellNet's brand, delivers incremental growth from new and existing customers, and manages all partner relationships with key suppliers. He was interviewed on Episode 30, "Leaders with Heart Strike a Balance between Confidence and Humility."

Alex Smith is the chief human resources officer and the chief change officer for the City of Memphis, where she works alongside almost eight thousand other city employees. Alex is the architect behind the city's talent management, training, employee relations, employee engagement, and diversity initiatives. She was interviewed on Episode 86, "Leaders with Heart Embrace Their People and Their Results."

Renée Smith is the founder and chief executive officer of A Human Workplace, a professional coaching company that inspires leaders to make workplaces more loving and human. Renée expands impact by providing a unique set of cultural resources for leaders, including learning experiences, ready-to-use tools, and consulting services. Prior to this role, she served as the first director of workplace transformation for the State of Washington, where she advocated for human-centered principles. She was interviewed on Episode 51, "Leaders with Heart Promote Love in the Workplace."

Ian Sohn is the president and chief client officer at Hawkeye, the largest customer-related-management (CRM) agency in North America, using empathic creativity and powerful technology to orchestrate unique experiences for people across their customer journey. Ian previously served as the CEO of Wunderman Thompson Central, where he oversaw all agency operations with an emphasis on expanding the agency's capabilities. He was interviewed on Episode 65, "Leaders with Heart Know They Must Give to Get and Grow."

Lon Southerland is the managing director of biomic sciences at Seraphic Group, Inc., a privately held, fast-growing biotechnology company committed to developing products that transform human health and the environment. Lon leads Seraphic Group's largest subsidiary to apply the rigor of cutting-edge science, the strength of humanity, and the intelligence of nature to transform our world. His mission is to raise the standards for what we put in our bodies and to improve the lives and health of humans. Lon was interviewed on Episode 90, "Leaders with Heart Remember Where They Came From."

Brent Stockwell is the assistant city manager for the City of Scottsdale, Arizona, which has a population of more than 250,000 citizens served by 2,500+ city employees. Brent is responsible for evidence-based decision-making and special projects, as well as overseeing the diversity and inclusion, communications, government relations, human resources, economic development, and tourism and events departments of the city, among others. He was interviewed on Episode 93, "Leaders with Heart Model Good Leadership."

Larry Sutton is the founder and president of RNR Tire Express, a national franchise retailer of quality tires and custom wheels. Under Larry's leadership, RNR has grown to more than 130 locations in twenty-six states with more than a thousand employees. He was interviewed on Episode 70, "Leaders with Heart Empower Their People to Do Their Best Work."

Gustavo Tavares is the country manager for Brazil at Top Employers Institute, a global authority on recognizing excellence in people practices by accelerating these practices to enrich the world of work. Gustavo leads a regional hub responsible for managing local and global Top Employers program participants across Latin America; developing new business opportunities; and ensuring the production and delivery of insightful, local-based content. He was interviewed on Episode 68, "Leaders with Heart Create a Culture of Autonomy."

Denise Testori is the president and CEO of Prestige Cleaners, an award-winning tailoring and garment cleaning operation employing more than sixty people across seven locations. Denise works with regulatory and legislative agencies on issues pertaining to the industry, helps lead Prestige's efforts to grow and expand pickup and delivery services, and helped lead the company to be one of the first dry cleaners in Arizona to embrace green practices. She was interviewed on Episode 26, "Leaders with Heart Know That They Must Lead the Whole Person."

D'anthony Tillery is the assistant vice president of talent acquisition at Atrium Health, a nationally recognized not-for-profit health care system with more than fifty-five thousand teammates at nearly forty hospitals and hundreds of care locations throughout the Carolinas and Georgia. D'anthony is committed to ensuring that the talent acquisition processes are effective, enabling the organization to meet the demands of an ever-changing marketplace. He was interviewed on Episode 43, "Leaders with Heart Lead with Compassion."

Rich Todd is the principal and chief executive officer of Innovest Portfolio Solutions, an independent and private provider of investment-related consulting services for benefit plans, nonprofits, and family offices supported by fifty-six employees. With more than thirty years of experience in investment consulting, Rich currently provides consulting services to both institutions and families. He is also a member of Innovest's Investment Committee, which makes decisions on investment related research. Rich was interviewed on Episode 8, "Leaders with Heart Are Servant Leaders Who Look at Their Role as a Vocation."

Kristi Turner is the chief marketing officer of Compeat Restaurant Management Software, a privately owned computer software company with more than two hundred employees, offering innovative restaurant management software. Using her decades of domestic and international strategic business experience, Kristi oversees product marketing strategy, competitive positioning, brand awareness, digital presence, customer retention, and internal and external communications. She was interviewed on Episode 14, "Leaders with Heart Don't Take Their Own Leadership for Granted."

Erik Van Bramer is senior vice president at the Federal Reserve Bank of Chicago, a banking nonprofit that serves the Seventh Federal Reserve District, an economically diverse region that includes all of Iowa and most of Illinois, Indiana, Michigan, and Wisconsin. As SVP, Erik serves the public interest by fostering a strong economy, promoting financial stability, and establishing an inclusive culture. He was interviewed on Episode 116, "Leaders with Heart Have Care as Their North Star."

Danielle Vaughan is the president of compliance at FirstBank, Colorado's second-largest depository institution and the state's largest locally owned and privately held bank, with a commitment to convenience and loyalty to its three thousand employees. Danielle previously served as the executive vice president of human resources, a role in which she oversaw many HR functions, including payroll, benefits, and employee relations. She was interviewed on Episode 58, "Leaders with Heart Know That They Are Works in Progress."

Greg Wathen is the president and chief executive officer of the Economic Development Coalition of Southwest Indiana, which facilitates business retention, expansion, and attraction activities, and supports efforts to enhance the business climate. Since March 2007, Greg's leadership has helped garner over $3.2 billion in investment, more than four thousand jobs, and $74 million in state and federal grants for the region. He was interviewed on Episode 67, "Leaders with Heart Naturally Think of Their People First."

Christina Wegner is the vice president of marketing for the Vollrath Company, a privately held company that leverages its reputation for high-quality engineering and manufacturing throughout its business divisions and 1,300 global employees. Christina has a demonstrated history of working in the financial services, plumbing, and sports industries. While they are all seemingly different industries, her role in building brands, fostering relationships, and developing people is the common thread in them all. She was interviewed on Episode 101, "Leaders with Heart Create Space for Open and Honest Feedback."

Megan Smiley Wick is the executive director of Gamma Phi Beta Sorority and Gamma Phi Beta Foundation, which strives to be a premier philanthropic organization supporting world-class leadership education for women of all identities. Megan is responsible for directing the operations of the Sorority and Foundation, including supervising an international workforce to carry out the goals of the Sorority's mission. She was interviewed on Episode 20, "Leaders with Heart Fill Their Calendar with Relationship-Building, Not Tasks."

DeeDee Williams is the director of human resources at Davis Graham & Stubbs LLP, a law practice with a national reputation for its work in the areas of corporate finance, natural resources, and energy, with a particular focus on complex commercial litigation and regulatory guidance. DeeDee oversees all of the firm's human resources functions, including benefits administration, staff recruitment and retention, workers' compensation, and labor and employment matters. She was interviewed on Episode 99, "Leaders with Heart Have a Strong Moral Compass."

Timbra Yoakum is the director of special programs for the Mabank Independent School District in Mabank, Texas. Timbra has been in education for fifteen years, spending the last eight as an educational diagnostician. She was interviewed on Episode 111, "Leaders with Heart Feel Called to Serve Others."

Notes

• • •

Introduction

1. Merriam-Webster.com, s.v. "caring," accessed August 28, 2020, https://www .merriam-webster.com/dictionary/caring.

Chapter 1

1. Simon Sinek, *Start with Why: How Great Leaders Inspire Everyone to Take Action* (New York: Portfolio/Penguin, 2009), 39.
2. Kristin Neff, "Definition of Self-Compassion," *Self-Compassion*, https://self -compassion.org/the-three-elements-of-self-compassion-2/.

Chapter 2

1. Liz Fosslien and Mollie West Duffy, "How Leaders Can Open Up to Their Teams Without Oversharing," *Harvard Business Review*, February 8, 2019, https://hbr .org/2019/02/how-leaders-can-open-up-to-their-teams-without-oversharing.

Chapter 3

1. Stephen R. Covey, *The 8th Habit: From Effectiveness to Greatness* (New York: Free Press, Illustrated Edition, 2005; Audible audio ed.), Introduction.

Chapter 5

1. Merriam-Webster.com, s.v. "accepted," accessed October 12, 2020, https://www .merriam-webster.com/dictionary/accepted.
2. Merriam-Webster.com, s.v. "empathy," accessed October 9, 2020, https://www .merriam-webster.com/dictionary/empathy.
3. Merriam-Webster.com, s.v. "compassion," accessed October 9, 2020, https:// www.merriam-webster.com/dictionary/compassion.

Chapter 7

1. Dan Harris, PhD, "Emotions in the Workplace: Creating an Emotional Safe Space," *Quantum Workplace*, June 18, 2019, https://www.quantumworkplace .com/future-of-work/emotions-in-the-workplace-creating-an-emotional-safe -space#.XzHrN1ZSKdM.email.

2. Amy C. Edmondson, *The Fearless Organization: Creating Psychological Safety in the Workplace for Learning, Innovation, and Growth* (Hoboken, NJ: John Wiley & Sons, 2018; Audible audio ed.), Introduction.

3. Derald Wing Sue, *Microaggressions in Everyday Life: Race, Gender and Sexual Orientation* (Hoboken, NJ: John Wiley & Sons, 2010), chapter 1.

Chapter 8

1. Merriam-Webster.com, s.v. "delegate," accessed October 9, 2020, https://www.merriam-webster.com/dictionary/delegate.

2. Merriam-Webster.com, s.v. "empower," accessed October 9, 2020, https://www.merriam-webster.com/dictionary/empower.

3. Merriam-Webster.com, s.v. "empowerment," accessed August 29, 2020, https://www.merriam-webster.com/dictionary/empowerment.

Chapter 9

1. Merriam-Webster Dictionary, s.v. "resilience," accessed August 29, 2020, https://www.merriam-webster.com/dictionary/resilience.

2. TedXColoradoSprings, July 23, 2019, https://www.youtube.com/watch?v=-bp4-IHyf50&feature=youtu.be).

3. Merriam-Webster.com, s.v. "reframe," accessed October 9, 2020, https://www.merriam-webster.com/dictionary/reframe.

Acknowledgments

• • •

To the Leadership With Heart team: Neil Hughes, for being the catalyst to light the flame underneath me to start my own podcast. I couldn't have done this without you. Emerald Rosal, who always manages to make me look better and smarter by contributing and crafting my show notes for the podcast. Nicole Gallicchio, thank you for supporting the service side of the podcast while interacting with podcast guests. All the leaders I have interviewed for the podcast and, by extension, this book. You are all highlighted in the appendix, but please know that you are also the highlight of many of my days. You help me see that the journey to becoming a caring leader is worth it.

To the Berrett-Koehler team: Steve Piersanti, thank you for your unwavering support of my voice and my work. I appreciate every piece of advice you gave me. Michael Crowley, thank you for your candid guidance on this book. Sohayla Farman, Elissa Rabellino, Leigh McLellan and team, thank you for making sure the book looked great! Maria Jesus Aguilo and Catherine Lengronne for making sure to position my book for the international market.

Adam Johnson, for producing a beautiful and memorable book design. Jeevan Sivasubramaniam, for selecting the best book reviewers and for being hospitable at my author day. Katie Sheehan, for getting the word out about my book and promoting it in all the right places. Tryn Brown, for working hard to sell the English version of my book internationally.

For those who reviewed my book to allow me to polish it and make it more accessible. Mitchell Friedman, Susan Hopp, Veronica Rabelo, I appreciate your generosity and foresight. In many ways, you help bring the best side of this work to life!

Paul Rohrer, thank you for being my sound engineer extraordinaire when recording the audiobook and Courtney Schonfeld for guiding me to create a stunning audiobook!

To the Employee Fanatix team: Thank you, Nikki Groom, Andrius Alvarez-Backus, Emerald Rosal, Niki Garcia, and Monica Thornton. Your help on driving the business forward allowed me to focus on writing this book.

To others who believe in me: Mike Vacanti Sr., you were the reason why I even found Berrett-Koehler as a publisher. You introduced me to Julie Winkle Giulioni, who was also a huge support and a burst of great insight. I reached out to Steve Piersanti right after our discussion, Mike, and he was gracious to give me his email directly. That sealed the deal, my friend. I adore the support I get from you.

To both Steve Paul and Rich Gassen, for being guests of the show but also my informal ambassadors for what I always hoped would be the impact of this show and this book. Kevin Kruse, who endorsed both my first book, *The 7 Intuitive Laws of Employee Loyalty*, and this book, despite the fact that we have never met, and he has been gracious in every way: thank you.

Chester Elton, we have never met, yet somehow we understand each other. I am thankful for the foreword you wrote for this book and for your uplifting and encouraging nature.

Ana De Magalhaes, you are such a light in my life. Loved you and your son when I met you in Brazil. I'm glad to call you my friend. Molly Smith, thank you for agreeing to endorse this book. Your openness to embrace my message is appreciated. Trisha Teig, PhD, I am honored that you agreed to review and endorse this book with the eye of an academic. You are wonderful!

Michele Nevarez, I will never forget our interaction on the podcast. We are so aligned, and I now am glad to call you my friend. Thank you for your endorsement. Dr. Paul Marciano, you are such a giving person. I so appreciate your openness to endorse my book while you were right in the middle of writing your own. Thank you!

To my closest friends, Sarah Elkins, Kimberly Davis, Melissa Hughes, and Ghislaine Bruner, without whose support during the crazy days of writing and writer's blocks this book would not be possible: many hugs!

To my family: I love you all so much, Luis, Gabriela, Sebastian, Dominic, and Matteo. Thank you for sticking with me and being patient while I wrote this book. Thanks, Gabriela, for not allowing me to rest on my laurels from the first book. It wasn't an easy road, but I hope you think it's worth it. You are my everything. Mom, you are always a great example of someone who leads with heart. I am glad you always choose to think of others first. Your caring leadership style helped me to form mine.

Index

• • •

About the Author

• • •

Heather Younger is a best-selling author, international speaker, consultant, adjunct organizational leadership professor, and facilitator who has earned her reputation as "The Employee Whisperer." Her experiences as an entrepreneur, manager, attorney, writer, coach, listener, speaker, collaborator, and mother all lend 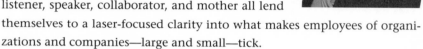 themselves to a laser-focused clarity into what makes employees of organizations and companies—large and small—tick.

Heather discovered her passion for caring leadership early on. As the only child from an interracial and interfaith marriage, she was excluded by certain members of her family. While it left her with questions growing up, it also led her to develop resilience, self-love, and a deep desire to advocate for the voiceless and create opportunities for people worldwide to learn strategies to reframe their own adversities in order to lead more satisfying lives.

As a champion for positive change in workplaces, communities, and our world at large, Heather founded Employee Fanatix, a leading employee engagement, diversity and inclusion, and leadership development consulting and training firm, to inspire others by teaching the kind of caring leadership that drives real business results.

During her time as CEO and founder, Heather has facilitated more than 350 workshops. Her motivation and philosophy has reached tens of thousands of attendees through her speaking engagements on large and small stages. Companies have charted their future course based on her focus groups, of which she has led nearly 100. In addition, she has helped companies see double-digit employee engagement score increases through implementation of her philosophies. She has driven results in a multitude of industries, including banking, oil and gas, construction, energy, healthcare, personal services, and federal and local government.

Heather hosts the weekly podcast *Leadership With Heart*, which uncovers what drives leaders from all over the world and all walks of life to be more emotionally intelligent leaders. Her book *The 7 Intuitive Laws of Employee Loyalty* hit the FORBES Must-Reads list and is a go-to source for HR professionals and organizational leaders seeking insight into their organization's dynamics. Heather is a Certified Diversity Professional, is certified in Emotional and Social Intelligence and DiSC™, and has a law degree from the University of Colorado Boulder Colorado Law school.

Heather lives in Aurora, Colorado, with her husband and four children. She enjoys hanging around with her crew. You may also find her trying to sneak into a movie all by herself for some peace and quiet.

You can learn more at **HeatherYounger.com**.

About Employee Fanatix

• • •

At Employee Fanatix, our purpose is simple: to equip companies and organizations with the intelligence they need to improve the quality of work life for their employees.

We are guided and inspired by our vision to help leaders shine by putting people at the heart of everything they do, while empowering employees with the knowledge that their voice and ideas matter.

As a leading employee engagement and leadership development consulting and training firm focused on helping companies and organizations to become more agile, creative, and successful, Employee Fanatix partners with in-house HR and management teams to uncover challenges and devise action plans to build trust, improve morale, and mitigate employee turnover.

By using innovative and effective listening and communication strategies, we unlock critical clues that reveal the source of ongoing problems and help leaders see those problems through a lens of opportunity.

Whether we're building a strategic plan to create a more inclusive workplace culture, delivering an effective employee communication strategy, coaching a leader to better engage and motivate his or her employees, or facilitating an employee focus group, everything we do is designed to uncover actionable insights that enable deep cultural improvements, increase leadership effectiveness, and drive business results.

You can learn more at **EmployeeFanatix.com.**

Berrett–Koehler
Publishers

Berrett-Koehler is an independent publisher dedicated to an ambitious mission: *Connecting people and ideas to create a world that works for all.*

Our publications span many formats, including print, digital, audio, and video. We also offer online resources, training, and gatherings. And we will continue expanding our products and services to advance our mission.

We believe that the solutions to the world's problems will come from all of us, working at all levels: in our society, in our organizations, and in our own lives. Our publications and resources offer pathways to creating a more just, equitable, and sustainable society. They help people make their organizations more humane, democratic, diverse, and effective (and we don't think there's any contradiction there). And they guide people in creating positive change in their own lives and aligning their personal practices with their aspirations for a better world.

And we strive to practice what we preach through what we call "The BK Way." At the core of this approach is *stewardship,* a deep sense of responsibility to administer the company for the benefit of all of our stakeholder groups, including authors, customers, employees, investors, service providers, sales partners, and the communities and environment around us. Everything we do is built around stewardship and our other core values of *quality, partnership, inclusion,* and *sustainability.*

This is why Berrett-Koehler is the first book publishing company to be both a B Corporation (a rigorous certification) and a benefit corporation (a for-profit legal status), which together require us to adhere to the highest standards for corporate, social, and environmental performance. And it is why we have instituted many pioneering practices (which you can learn about at www.bkconnection.com), including the Berrett-Koehler Constitution, the Bill of Rights and Responsibilities for BK Authors, and our unique Author Days.

We are grateful to our readers, authors, and other friends who are supporting our mission. We ask you to share with us examples of how BK publications and resources are making a difference in your lives, organizations, and communities at www.bkconnection.com/impact.

Dear reader,

Thank you for picking up this book and welcome to the worldwide BK community! You're joining a special group of people who have come together to create positive change in their lives, organizations, and communities.

What's BK all about?

Our mission is to connect people and ideas to create a world that works for all.

Why? Our communities, organizations, and lives get bogged down by old paradigms of self-interest, exclusion, hierarchy, and privilege. But we believe that can change. That's why we seek the leading experts on these challenges—and share their actionable ideas with you.

A welcome gift

To help you get started, we'd like to offer you a **free copy** of one of our bestselling ebooks:

www.bkconnection.com/welcome

When you claim your **free ebook**, you'll also be subscribed to our blog.

Our freshest insights

Access the best new tools and ideas for leaders at all levels on our blog at ideas.bkconnection.com.

Sincerely,

Your friends at Berrett-Koehler

Certified

Corporation